"We're Going to See the Beatles!"

An Oral History of Beatlemania as Told by the Fans Who Were There

Garry Berman

SANTA
MONICA
PRESS

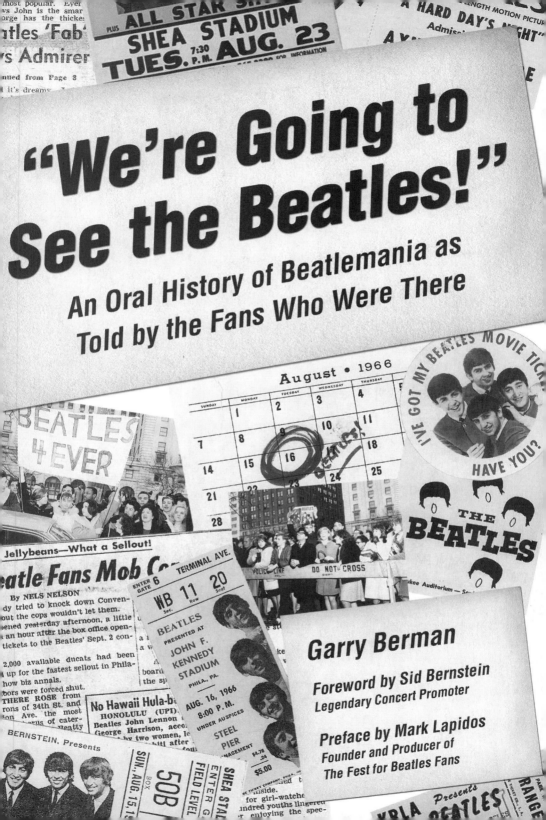

"We're Going to See the Beatles!"

An Oral History of Beatlemania as Told by the Fans Who Were There

Garry Berman

Foreword by Sid Bernstein
Legendary Concert Promoter

Preface by Mark Lapidos
*Founder and Producer of
The Fest for Beatles Fans*

Published by: Santa Monica Press LLC
P.O. Box 1076
Santa Monica, CA 90406-1076
1-800-784-9553
www.santamonicapress.com
books@santamonicapress.com

Printed in the United States

Santa Monica Press books are available at special quantity discounts when purchased in bulk by corporations, organizations, or groups. Please call our Special Sales department at 1-800-784-9553.

ISBN-13 978-1-59580-032-9
ISBN-10 1-59580-032-8

Library of Congress Cataloging-in-Publication Data

Berman, Garry.
  We're going to see the Beatles! : an oral history of Beatlemania as told by the fans who were there / by Garry Berman ; foreword by Sid Bernstein ; preface by Mark Lapidos.
    p. cm.
  ISBN 978-1-59580-032-9
  1. Beatles. 2. Rock music fans—Interviews. I. Title.
ML421.B4B52 2008
782.42166092'2—dc22

2008001800

Cover and interior design and production by cooldogdesign

Beatles photos by PoPsie ©2008 by Michael Randolph
www.popsiephotos.com

Contents

Jumpin' Jellybeans—What a Se

Beatle Fans Me

By NELS NELSON

Somebody tried to knock down Conven
tion Hall, but the cops wouldn't let them.

It happened yesterday afternoon, a litt
more than an hour after the box office ope
ed to sell tickets to the Beatles' Sept. 2 cc
cert.

The 12,000 available ducats had be
whooshed up for the fastest sellout in Ph
delphia show biz annals.

The doors were forced shut.

AND THERE ROSE from
the environs of 34th St. and
Convention Ave. the most
--rendous chorus of cater-
ince Clyde Beatty
s butcher and
s on watercress

No Hav

HON(
Beatles
George
panied
Hawai
brief v
squeal
watch

00 teenaged fe-
d in scorned fury.
or more collapsed
avention Hall steps
Others battered at the doo
s of St. Trinian's. A pincers
tacked the trade entrance

few brave ones rat-a-tatted th
cops' chests.

LITTLE BLONDE in green
ts ran up to the wall and

FOREWORD

Promoting the Beatles, Meeting the Fans

by SID BERNSTEIN
Legendary Concert Promoter

As a soldier in World War II, I was stationed for a while—before we went into tougher terrain—in England. I fell in love with the country. I like the people, I like the civility that I experienced in London and in the countryside, and I just fell in love with every blade of grass—that green, beautiful grass.

I finally came home in one piece, back to my family, and still thinking of England. I started to read an English newspaper here. These days, every fifth newsstand in Manhattan has a newspaper from England, but at that time, you had to go to the out-of-town newsstand on 42nd Street and Times Square. I'd get the English paper to read about the government and what was going on in my second most favorite country. And here I am, probably one of the few Americans picking it up every week.

Once, years later, my eye stopped for a moment to read just one or two paragraphs, one column wide, about four boys creating a sensation in Liverpool. They were playing lunchtime at a place called the Cavern, which was four or five blocks from where Brian Epstein had a little record shop.

I called Brian, who was still living with his mom in Liverpool, and I asked him for a date we could arrange for a Beatles concert here. Brian at first said, "I don't want to play my boys there, they're very popular here and I'm getting all sorts of offers. I don't want them playing to an empty house." We finally agreed and made a deal for Carnegie Hall, to take place on February 12th, 1964. He said, "I won't come in until we have at least one hit record." I had to wait until that hit record happened, which was around October of 1963. By the time my day rolled around, my tickets had taken on new importance. Ed Sullivan then booked the Beatles for Sunday, February 9th, three days before my show at Carnegie Hall. So here they are playing on the *Sullivan* show, and also doing my show three days later, and having achieved the number one song by then. So my tickets, which were priced at $3.50, $4.50, and $5.50, sold out in a half hour at the box office. And they were selling for up to about $500.00 a ticket on the street.

After Carnegie Hall, I heard from the box office manager, Nat Posnik, who said, "You could've played them for fifty days, Sid, and sold out the house for fifty days." I called Brian overseas, and said, "Brian, we had talked about the possibility of playing Madison Square Garden. I want to change that."

"Where do you want to play them, Sid?"

"I want to put them in Shea Stadium."

Brian was concerned again about the Beatles possibly playing to empty seats in a stadium with 55,000 seats. I said, "Brian, I'll give you ten dollars for every empty seat there is." We had established a nice relationship after Carnegie Hall, so he said, "If you're that sure, Sid." We had done Carnegie on a handshake, and we did Shea Stadium on a handshake, too.

But the *second* Shea concert, in 1966, didn't sell out. One reason? The Singer sewing machine.

I had the opportunity to work with Tony Bennett, who had done a TV show sponsored by Singer. The vice president of Singer told me the company was opening a new store at Rockefeller Center, right above the rink. I liked him and wanted to help him with the promotion. I told him I'd sell him several thousand tickets for the Shea concert for face value, for him to put on sale at the store. He became the main outlet. My babysitters were counting the tickets with me to take to him. We had to count off about 18,000 tickets. We put them in cigar boxes, shoe boxes . . . A year after the event, I found a box full of tickets— about 2,500 tickets that we didn't send down to Singer. And that was the reason there was a big space of empty seats in Shea stadium at the concert.

The Beatles made me an international *semi*-celebrity. People know me wherever I go. Some want me to run for office. But if nominated, I will not run!

My impression of Beatles fans hasn't changed. Once stung by a Beatle, you are stung forever. I meet faces with the same smile, with similar interests, and with the same enthusiasm among young people who have become Beatles fans, as well as the 40-year-olds and gray-haired fans. They're all pretty much the same: decent, fun-loving, and, almost without exception, if I meet a Beatles fan, I like them. It's like a society, a sorority—we all come from the same university. The university of love.

— Sid Bernstein

The Beatles, In My Life

by MARK LAPIDOS

Founder and Producer of The Fest for Beatles Fans

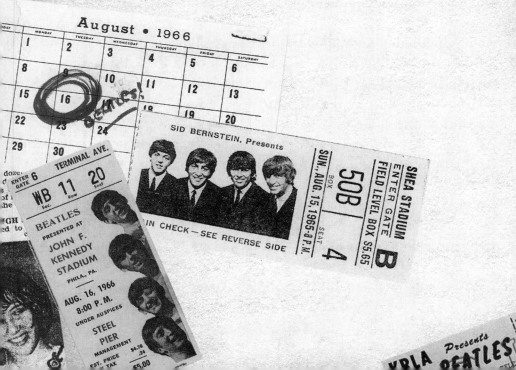

It was January 6, 1964. It was a Monday evening, around a quarter to 8:00. I was listening to WABC-AM and the *Scott Muni Show*. I was sitting on my bed, after the first day back at school from the two-week Christmas break, and I heard this song, "I Want to Hold Your Hand." Muni didn't announce who it was, or perhaps I wasn't listening. But all of a sudden, I sat up and said, "What is this?" I got so excited about it, and after the song Muni said, "That's a group from England called the Beatles." What a strange name. But I absolutely loved the song. It was so different, and such an exciting song, it really grabbed me that first moment—and hasn't let go since.

The next day I came home from school, and Tuesday was the new Survey Day on WABC, and "I Want to Hold Your Hand" was number one. So I went from hearing it for the first time the previous evening to learning it was number one the next day. I was hooked on the Beatles from the very beginning. My birthday is in January, so my brother bought me *Introducing the Beatles* (*Meet the Beatles* wasn't out yet). It was the first album I ever owned. Two weeks later they were on *The Ed Sullivan Show*, and the rest is history.

For the second *Sullivan* show, I was in Florida, for the Washington's birthday holiday, as we called it back then. My parents took me to Miami Beach, where we stayed at the Casablanca Hotel. One day my mother and I were walking down Collins Avenue, and I see the Deauville Hotel, just about two blocks away. That's where the Beatles were staying! There was a crowd of people gathered, and I found out that the Beatles were going to be leaving soon. I took a guess that they were going to be leaving from the alley, which they did, and I got right up to their limo, knocked on the window and waved to them, and I ran down Collins Avenue with them for about 20 seconds.

Ten years later, I was manager at the flagship Sam Goody music store at Radio City Music Hall. While there, at the end of 1973, I got the idea that somebody should do something to celebrate the 10th anniversary of the Beatles' arrival in America. And the word "Beatlefest" just popped into my head (it's now called "The Fest for Beatles Fans"). I had a vision of people gathering in a hotel to watch Beatles films, listening to their music, trading memorabilia, and a bunch of other things. I sat with the idea for about a month or so, then I decided give it a try. I took money from my own savings to book the Commodore Hotel for September 7th and 8th of that year, and I wrote to all of the Beatles— I wasn't going to do the show without their support. Of course, everybody thought I was nuts. How was I going to get their support while they're suing each other? But that didn't stop me.

I hadn't heard from anybody until I learned that John Lennon and Harry Nilsson were going to be appearing in Central Park for a March of Dimes walk-a-thon. They weren't playing, just speaking to raise awareness for the charity. To make a long story short, I found out where John was staying, found out his room number, went to the hotel and up to his room, and knocked on the door. Harry Nilsson, who later became a dear friend, opened the door. I said, "Hi, I'm Mark Lapidos, and I'd like to speak to John about Beatlefest." He waved me in, and I said hello to John, sat down, and told him my idea about the Fest. He said, "I'm all for it. I'm a Beatles fan too." And he got very excited about it. I mentioned that I wanted to do a charity raffle. He offered to donate a signed guitar. Two days later I'm sitting with his people talking it out with Apple in London. Within a couple of days, I got signed drumsticks from Ringo, and it took off from there.

Getting the logistics for the show set up was not easy. I left Sam Goody three weeks before the show. They knew I was doing it, and they supported me, but I just had to put every minute of the day into it. At lunchtimes I'd take a roll of dimes, walk two blocks to the Hilton, and sit in the phone booth for an hour and just make phone calls, and grab a hot dog on the way back. It was a major undertaking.

A few days before the Fest, Tony King from Apple was in the States, and asked if I had received anything autographed from Paul or George. I said I hadn't heard from them. He went over to John, and John called Paul and George and reminded them that they hadn't yet sent anything to Beatlefest. Apparently my messages hadn't reached them, so John arranged to get a few signed things from them right away, and we soon had items from all four Beatles for the show.

On the Saturday of the show, Tony told me that John wanted to come down the next night to pick out the winning raffle name for his signed guitar. I didn't tell a soul. Rumors were flying, and it was the biggest secret I ever had to keep. But I guess he heard how crowded it was, and got cold feet. It was very close.

We've held over 100 Fests since that first one. It's wonderful to see another generation of fans. My children are Beatles fans, and so are their friends—they're part of our staff, and they love the show. Parents come with their 5- and 6-year-olds, who are already wearing Beatles T-shirts. There's also a couple from Pennsylvania who used to come every year, now they come every few years, who are well into their seventies. Sometimes they come with their kids, sometimes by themselves. And the teenagers who come hear the Beatles' music, and they know whatever else they listen to now doesn't even touch what the Beatles did.

They hear the difference.

— Mark Lapidos

Introduction

I was born in 1961, and apparently, from what my family tells me, became a Beatles fan in 1964. I vaguely remember dancing to and singing—not long after I learned to talk, and possibly before—"I Want to Hold Your Hand" and "I Saw Her Standing There" in the basement, as the 45s spun on a portable record player. In all honesty, however, I can't really consider myself a part of the original generation of Beatles fans. So, I've often wondered what it was like to be a teenage Beatles fan as Beatlemania exploded across America. What was it like to watch the same-day TV reports of the group arriving in New York, or to be one of those screaming teenagers lined along the streets of major American cities, straining to get a glimpse of the Beatles in their limousine speeding past? What was it like to wait for new issues of the Beatles' fan magazines on candy store racks, or feeling an almost unbearable anticipation waiting to hear Beatles songs debut on the radio?

Sometime in the early 1990s, an item came into my possession that gave me a truly tangible clue as to what it meant to be a part of Beatlemania. My parents returned from a trip to New York State and, having stopped in several antique shops along the way, brought home a few presents for me. One of these was an old scrapbook, with a green vinyl cover and black construction paper pages. Each one of those pages was filled with articles and pictures from many different newspapers covering just about every move the Beatles made throughout 1964 and '65. Each and every clipping was painstakingly and lovingly cut and glued onto the scrapbook pages by a girl who had lived and breathed the Beatles throughout that special time of her life. She obviously spent hours combing through every newspaper and magazine she could lay her hands on, snipping out any story, photo, or blurb that either featured the Beatles, or merely mentioned them in passing. She didn't miss much, from the movie ads for *A Hard Day's Night* and *Help!,* to the *TV Guide* listings for the group's first appearance on *The Ed Sullivan Show*. It's a fascinating, even breathtaking piece of pop culture history.

Now I was beginning to get it. *This* is what it was like! For millions of teenagers at the time, the Beatles were all-consuming. Teenage girls traded Beatles fan magazines in the same way that boys traded baseball cards—and, truth be told, the boys began to take an interest in those magazines as well.

As unlikely as it may seem, these very same obsessed young fans would, less than five years later, become what could arguably be called "The Second Greatest Generation"(with apologies to Tom Brokaw). They are the sons and daughters of parents who had grown up during the Great Depression, and fought two fronts of a world war simultaneously on opposite sides of the globe. After World War II, millions of young G.I. vets and their wives settled down in newly created suburbs, buying $5,000 homes, and eager to start a life raising the first generation of baby boomers.

These boomers, specifically those born within a few years on either side of 1950, would, as children entering their teens, experience the nationwide shock of seeing a president assassinated. Only half a decade later, in their college years, they would discover the power of social and political activism. It would lead them to seek, with passion and resolve, an end to the Vietnam War, an end to racial and sexual discrimination, an end to uncontrolled pollution and environmental damage, and ultimately an end to the most scandal-ridden presidency in American history.

For all of the internal conflict America experienced throughout the 1960s—it would not be an exaggeration to consider those years our second Civil War—the changes in lifestyles and attitudes triggered by that passion of the baby boomer generation have lingered for decades.

In late 1963, however, the young boomers' world was very different. While global situations such as the Cold War and the space race were on the front pages and on the evening news as a matter of daily routine, kids in their early teens also had their own, somewhat insular world in which to thrive. As always, entertainment in its many forms was a top priority.

On television, there were all of three networks to choose from, plus one or two local stations in larger cities. The top-rated show in the country at the time was *The Beverly Hillbillies*, although younger viewers might have identified more closely with the teenage machinations of Patty Duke in her new sitcom, *The Patty Duke Show*. Other favorites included *The Fugitive*, *The Dick Van Dyke Show*, and *The Twilight Zone*. And few of these programs were likely to come in clearly without the rabbit ears on top of the TV set adjusted at just the right angles.

For those who enjoyed an evening out at the movies (preferably at the drive-in), the films of 1963 included: *Bye Bye Birdie*, *The Nutty Professor*, James Bond's second cinematic adventure *From Russia With Love*, Alfred Hitchcock's *The Birds*, and the comedy spectacular *It's A Mad, Mad, Mad, Mad World* (released just one week before President Kennedy's assassination).

And then there was pop music, pouring from Top 40 stations and forever testing the life span of transistor radio batteries across the land. Among the top songs of 1963 were "He's So Fine" (the Chiffons), "Go Away Little Girl" (Steve Lawrence), "It's My Party" (Leslie Gore), "My Boyfriend's Back" (The Angels), "Surf City" (Jan & Dean), and "Walk Like A Man" (The Four Seasons).

So far, so good—but also so bland. The songs individually were fine, and are still emanating from oldies radio stations to this day. But collectively, there wasn't much on the radio to get truly excited about in 1963. Teenaged pop music aficionados may have been hoping for a new jolt of excitement right around that time, but they didn't expect the jolt to be a lightning bolt sent by four young men called the Beatles, hailing from the far-away seaport town of Liverpool, England.

The Beatles' historic appearance on *The Ed Sullivan Show* was seen by a then record of 73 million viewers. The boomer generation comprised about 40% of the population in the U.S., including almost 22 million teenagers between the ages of 13–18. By the time the Beatles made that first appearance, the vast majority of those 22 million teenage boomers, mostly females, had fallen hopelessly in love with the rock group from Liverpool, England that was about to conquer America's popular culture.

This book is not about uncovering new, intimate details about the Beatles' lives that only the most inside of insiders could possibly have known. This is an oral history about—and told by—the first generation of Beatles fans, i.e., those teenage baby boomers who felt that lightning bolt hit on February 9, 1964, and became infatuated with the Fab Four—just like the girl who put together that wonderful scrapbook. The recollections on the following pages revisit the era through the eyes and ears of over 40 of these fans, who have shared their memories from all across the country. It is as much about this first baby-boomer generation and how the Beatles influenced their young lives (and, in many cases, their *entire* lives) as it is about the Beatles themselves.

These pages include stories from those who witnessed the Beatles' first arrival at Kennedy Airport in 1964, who kept vigil for them outside the Plaza Hotel, and who sat in the studio audience of *The Ed Sullivan Show* during the group's landmark first live TV broadcast here. Other contributors describe their rather creative attempts to meet the Beatles at the hotels in which they stayed on tour, or finding ways to attend their press conferences without getting thrown out. Still more talk about being in the stands of the historic Shea Stadium concert, while others contribute memories of over 20 different concerts the Beatles performed across the country between 1964 and 1966. Along the way, classic pop culture items of that period are also recalled with great nostalgia: portable record players, penny loafers, Instamatic cameras, and, of course, Beatles souvenirs.

"We're Going to See the Beatles!," as it documents a unique period in the lives of this generation, benefits from the participants' hindsight and life experience as they re-create—with considerable humor, and even passion—what it was like to have their young lives turned upside down by the biggest rock group of all time.

This book is dedicated to Beatles fans of all generations, everywhere.

— Garry Berman

The Contributors

eet the interviewees for this book, who so graciously do-nated their time, their photos, and their cherished memories:

Kathy Albinder attended the Forest Hills, New York concert on August 28, 1964, and met the Beatles during her quick sneak into the lobby of the Warwick Hotel in Manhattan the day before the Shea Stadium concert in 1965.

Barbara Allen sat in the press box with her friends for the Beatles' Philadelphia concert on September 2, 1964.

Linda Andriot saw the Cincinnati concert with her sister at Crosley Field on August 21, 1966.

Leslie Barratt joined the crowd of thousands waiting for the Beatles outside the Plaza Hotel during their first visit in February 1964.

Barbara Boggiano was a big teenage fan, but, much to her dismay, wasn't allowed to attend the famous Shea Stadium concert.

Paul Chasman, a professional musician, arrived at one of the Hollywood Bowl concerts in August 1965 with a friend mainly to look at girls, and left a hopelessly devoted Beatles fan.

Mary Ann Collins camped out overnight with her friends in front of a movie theatre in Newport News, Virginia, to be the first to buy tickets for the premiere of *A Hard Day's Night*.

Linda Cooper grew up in Maryland and attended three Beatles concerts in three different cities in 1964, 1965, and 1966.

Carol Cox attended the Beatles concert at San Francisco's Cow Palace on August 31, 1965.

Douglas Edwards became a Beatles fan in Ohio when he was just 11 years old.

Dale Ford saw the Beatles three times in San Francisco, including their last concert ever, on August 29, 1966.

Ilona Gabriel saw the Beatles at Shea Stadium and kept the Beatlemania spirit alive with her friends at Beatles rallies in the years after the group's touring ended.

June Harvey was in the studio audience of the Beatles' first historic appearance on *The Ed Sullivan Show.*

Pete Kennedy, a professional musician and performer, saw the Beatles' 1966 concert in Washington, D.C.

Claudia Kilburn went to the Seattle concert on August 21, 1964.

Lila Kraai attended a Beatles press conference with her friends in San Francisco, where they gave the group the key to the city of Los Gatos.

Claire Krusch saw the Beatles' Atlantic City concert on August 30, 1964.

Maryanne Laffin attended the Shea Stadium concerts in 1965 and '66.

Janet Lessard received a free ticket to the Beatles' Boston concert on September 12, 1964 by offering to write a review for her local newspaper.

Debbie Levitt, possibly the *first* American Beatles fan, lives and breathes the Beatles to this day; attended several of their concerts during the Beatlemania era, and almost all of their solo concerts in the U.S. and abroad.

Paula Lewis celebrated her 14th birthday by excitedly watching the Beatles' first appearance on *The Ed Sullivan Show,* and has been a fan ever since.

Linda Binns Liles, as a nine-year-old, met and chatted with all four Beatles, spending most of her time with Ringo, on the train taking the group from New York to their first U.S. concert in Washington, D.C. Her time with them was filmed and included in Albert Maysles' famous documentary of the Beatles' first U.S. visit.

JoAnne McCormack a lifelong, diehard fan, saw the Beatles at both Shea Stadium concerts (and can be seen screaming for them in the official 1965 Shea concert film), as well as Forest Hills. She also got into trouble in her Catholic school by declaring in public, "I'd rather see the Beatles than see the Pope."

Cathy McCoy-Morgan attended the concert at Convention Hall in Philadelphia on September 2, 1964, and the concert at JFK Stadium in Philadelphia on August 16, 1966.

Deborah McDermott saw the Beatles' 1966 concert in Washington, D.C.

Suzanne Milstead attended the Beatles' 1964 concert in Atlantic City.

Harold Montgomery attended the Beatles concert at Suffolk Downs racetrack in Massachusetts on August 18, 1966.

Carol Moore saw the Beatles in concert in Atlantic City, and attended their charity concert at the Paramount Theatre in New York City on September 20, 1964.

Art Murray, a New Jersey native, was skeptical of the Beatles at first, but became a big fan with a deep appreciation of their influence on his generation throughout the 1960s.

Paula Myers attended the Beatles' press conference in San Francisco as well as their concert there on August 31, 1965.

Carolyn Long Paulk attended the Dallas concert on September 18, 1964.

Charles Pfeiffer, as a young fan, was denied permission to attend the Beatles' September 1964 Kansas City concert after an argument with his mother.

David Rauh is a lifelong fan and collector of Beatles records from all over the world.

Jim Rugino became a fan at first sight during the Beatles' first appearance on *The Ed Sullivan Show.*

Betty Taucher saw the Beatles at their Cleveland concert on August 14, 1966, where fans rushed the stage, bringing the show to a temporary halt.

Wendi Tisland took a bus from northern Minnesota to see the Beatles' concert in Minneapolis on August 21, 1965.

Brian Tourville attended the group's Boston concert in 1964.

Valerie Volponi saw the Beatles at their Forest Hills concert in 1964, and attended both Shea Stadium concerts.

Penny Wagner, a lifelong fan and part-time chauffeur, drove Ringo and his band to their hotel in Milwaukee during his tour in 2003.

Annette Joseph Walker, along with her friends, stole maid uniforms in an attempt to sneak into the Plaza Hotel during the Beatles' first visit to New York. She also attended the August 23, 1966 Shea concert.

Shaun Weiss may be the only living person to have attended not only the Beatles' first live appearance on *The Ed Sullivan Show*, but also their first Shea Stadium concert, *and* their famous rooftop concert seen in the film *Let It Be*. Befriended Beatles roadie Mal Evans and became a "go-fer" for them in London during 1969–'70.

Maggie Welch saw the Beatles at the Red Rocks outdoor amphitheater in Colorado on August 26, 1964.

the most popular. Eyer
knows John is the smar
George has the thickes

Beatles 'Fab'
says Admirer

Continued from Page 3
r, and it's ⬦

PLUS ALL ST R
SHEA STADIUM
TUES. 7:30 AUG. 23
P.M.

A HARD DAY'S M
Admis

CHAPTER ONE

Early Rumblings

SID BERNSTEIN, Presents

BEATLES
PRESENTED AT
JOHN F.
KENNEDY
STADIUM
PHILA., PA.
AUG. 16, 1966
8:00 P.M.
UNDER AUSPICES
STEEL
PIER
MANAGEMENT
EST. PRICE $4.76
TAX .24
$5.00

TERMINAL AVE.
ENTER GATE 6
WB 11 20
Sec. Row Seat

August • 1966

IN CHECK — SEE REVERSE SIDE

SHEA STADIUM
ENTER GATE B
FIELD LEVEL BOX $5.65
BOX 50B
SEAT 4
SUN., AUG. 15, 1965-8 P.M.

As the autumn days of 1963 grew shorter and colder, rock & roll was less than a decade old, and experiencing some growing pains. Bill Haley and the Comets had the first rock & roll #1 hit, "Rock Around the Clock" in 1955. With the new era came the likes of Little Richard, Chuck Berry, Jerry Lee Lewis, Buddy Holly, Fats Domino, and others who sprang to the forefront with their own blends of blues, R&B, and country set to danceable and up-tempo beats. Elvis Presley quickly soared above them all in terms of popularity. But this era was in fact short-lived. Elvis was inducted into the Army in March of 1958, and many say his post-army music never recaptured its early edge. Chuck Berry and Jerry Lee Lewis began to have run-ins with the law—never a good selling point for the parents of teenage fans. In 1959, established star Buddy Holly and promising new favorites Richie Valens and J.P. "The Big Bopper" Richardson all died in a small plane crash while on tour together (the tragedy became known as "The Day the Music Died," immortalized in Don McLean's opus "American Pie" in 1972).

The first rock & roll craze, with all of its liberating—and to some, threatening—energy, had already come and gone by 1963. Even the doo-wop groups so popular in the late '50s were finding their life expectancy surprisingly brief—only one or two hits per group, if they were lucky. The next few years saw a backlash against the rebellious rock & roll, and the rise of innocuous, clean-cut, young pop singers whose very blandness posed no threat (imagined or otherwise) to the parents of the first baby-boomer generation. Groups like Frankie Valli and the Four Seasons, as well as some of Motown's "girl groups," managed to successfully create a hybrid sound of doo-wop and rock & roll. Overall, though, the American music scene in 1963 was coming up short in genuine excitement among the industry's youngest, most ardent and knowledgeable followers. It was this generation of 13- to 17-year-olds that would soon prove, with breathtaking swiftness and power, how influential they could be in determining the new course of American popular culture.

* * *

Barbara Allen: In that time period, we had missed all the Elvis excitement 'cause we were little kids in the '50s. So, my cousins, who were older and more sophisticated, had gone through the Elvis craze that I had missed out on. We were raised on the pure R&B, rock & roll, and from a young age I loved all that music. Of course, then in the early '60s, it was all Bobby Darren, the Four Seasons, the girl groups like the Shirelles, the Chiffons, Brenda Lee. . . . And we were kids who were brought up in a Bucks County, Pennsylvania suburb, so it was somewhat upper middle class, all the fathers were business people and professionals. So our exposure was really limited pretty much to TV or perhaps what we got through the radio. We weren't, say, in a city environment, where we would be taken by maybe an older sibling into a club where we'd hear jazz or blues or that kind of music. This was interesting for me 'cause this started me on a road to a love of music that I had only experienced through American rock & roll.

Paul Chasman: When I was younger I was really into Elvis, and I guess it wasn't until later that I could distinguish between the raw Elvis, before he went into the service, and the kind of watered down Elvis that came out after. And then at that time the sort of watered down wannabes came along. That whole Frankie Avalon, Fabian, Bobby Rydell thing, that was all real bland, milquetoast. When you're a kid listening to the radio it all sort of blends into the fabric, like wallpaper, part of the atmosphere that you grow up in. But I remember also at that time there was some cool stuff going on with some of the girl groups, some of the black music coming out then.

* * *

At this same time, there was something happening in the seaport city of Liverpool, England that began to spark the interest of rock music lovers there. The city was swarming with aspiring rock & roll groups with varying degrees of talent, who were combining their English folk music style called "Skiffle" with the early American rock & roll they had been hearing from records brought back from the States by local seamen.

To make a long and much-repeated story short, a particular Liverpool group called the Beatles was fast becoming established as the group to see in that city. At this time, Americans—and even most Britons—didn't yet have a clue as to what was about to happen. Perceptive observers, however, saw something special about the Beatles. In a very few instances, word about them began to trickle out of England and make it to America.

And, if it is possible for a single individual to have been the first Beatles fan in America, Debbie Levitt could easily stake that claim. She became a Beatles fan in 1962 in her native New York City, thanks to a pen pal in Liverpool who regularly reported to her about the charismatic group playing afternoon sets at a dingy Liverpool club called The Cavern Club.

* * *

Debbie Levitt: My school had a pick-a-pen-pal thing. So we were given different places to pick, and what do you think I picked? I picked Liverpool. Where the hell is it? I had no clue. So I had this pen pal in Liverpool, and we'd correspond—this was in '61, '62. And she's telling me how she goes with the lunchtime crowd to this place called the Cavern, and she sees this band that's got long hair that's really wild, and plays American rock & roll, and it's really something. She says to me, "I knew they were gonna be big as far as their success goes, 'cause you could see them radiate on the stage how great they were. It wasn't just an afternoon pop band, it wasn't Rory Storm and it wasn't Gerry and the Pacemakers, it was something with the four of them—it was just watching them that made you say, 'This is going to go far.'"

She was my eyes and my ears there. I was living through her. So she mails me records, articles, everything that she has. She mailed me the 45s, and I was able to listen and understand it, and it took so long for the letters to get back and forth. I said, "Mail me, mail me! If you can record it, record it!" She didn't, 'cause that would have been the incredible thing of the century. Can you imagine a home tape of it?

So I was a fan before anybody in this country really caught on to it.

* * *

By the first few months of 1963, the Beatles were sweeping the young people of Britain off their feet. Their first album, *Please Please Me*, was recorded in a single day—February 11, 1963—and released in Britain on March 22nd. The rest of 1963 became a whirlwind for the group, as their popularity seemed to grow exponentially by the week.

By late autumn, Beatlemania had begun to surge across the Atlantic, taking over the hearts, minds, and entire lives of American teenagers. But was there a precise moment or event to mark the flash point of the phenomenon? There are actually a few from which to choose, and each fan had his or her own Beatles-induced epiphany, the moment of first becoming aware of the group's very existence.

It isn't easy to make sense of the chronology of those early Beatles releases that first caught the ear of American listeners in late 1963. One reason is that the group's early British singles and albums rarely appeared both in Britain and the U.S. at the same time, and in the same order of release. Some Beatles 45s were delayed before their release in America, while others were released here with B-sides different than those on the British versions. Confusing? It gets worse. The first Beatles LP, *Please Please Me*, was released in the U.K. and Europe in March of 1963, and their second album, *With the Beatles*, was released later that year, on the fateful November 22nd. However, the first American Beatles album, *Meet the Beatles*, combined selected songs from those first two British LPs and was released in January of '64 (more about that later). Further adding to the confusion, smaller independent labels such as Vee-Jay and Swan acquired and released early singles such as "Please Please Me" and "She Loves You" without much of an

The Beatles returned to the grungy Cavern in the spring of '63, even after becoming nationwide stars in the U.K.

initial response by the public. But the presence of those first tangible sounds and images of the group began to grow throughout early autumn of '63.

* * *

Paul Chasman: The first time I heard the Beatles I was home sick from school. I don't remember what song it was, but even then they had such a unique sound, and I was really drawn to them, but at the same time didn't have any concept of their significance. I remember feeling a little bit resistant to them because they sounded so different. Just the blend of their voices was different than anything I had ever heard before. Structurally, the way their songs were put together, which now as a musician I can analyze and say, whoa, they were really doing some creative things that hadn't been done until that time. But at the time all I knew was that it was a different sound.

Paula Myers: We liked the Beatles when they had that song "Please Please Me," when it first came out. That was pretty early on. We heard it before they had released anything else, in fact we didn't know it was the Beatles. We liked the song a lot and we thought it was the Everly Brothers, until we discovered later that it was actually the Beatles.

* * *

It's hardly surprising, then, that few of *Time* magazine's readers were likely to take much notice of a four-paragraph story in the November 15, 1963 issue about a craze that had been sweeping across Britain's teenage music scene. In those days, British life was a bit of an enigma to the average American. Britain meant funny accents, Big Ben, the Queen, double-decker buses, and, to some, perhaps Peter Sellers or James Bond films. There was not as fluid an exchange of popular culture, specifically television or music, taking place between the two countries in the early '60s as there is today. Anything British then was still a bit of an exotic curiosity to us Yanks.

In that context, the *Time* article introduced us to a rock group called the Beatles, reporting that "their songs consist mainly of 'Yeh!' screamed to the accompaniment of three guitars and a thunderous drum." An amusing act, the story reported, but not such a big deal. However, *Time's* rival *Newsweek* included a similar piece about the long-haired musicians the very next week (the repeated emphasis placed on their hair length is difficult to fathom today). Network news programs offered brief clips of them in performance, but perhaps even more noteworthy than their music was the hysterical reactions by their fans. Curiosity, peppered with a growing sense of genuine interest in this foursome from Liverpool, began to take hold.

Then, suddenly, the nation was thrown into a state of shock on November 22, 1963, with the assassination of President Kennedy.

* * *

Janet Lessard: And all of us of my age will always re-member where we were when Kennedy was killed. I was at parochial school, so they obviously announced it over the loudspeaker and we went home. By the time we got home at 3:00 it was announced that he was dead. And it was a somber time in the whole country. Our parents were quite stricken by this, because it really did affect a lot of people when Kennedy was shot. That was a very painful time for a lot of people. And I think that might have been part of it. When the Beatles, so different, landed on the scene, it was almost like we were ready to accept something a little bit lighter and kind of took our mind off things.

Jim Rugino: Part of it was the grief reaction to Kennedy. That was the first time after Kennedy's death that any of us thought there was going to be a future . . . and that's I think a lot of what they represented. It was just this rush of excitement. I think it was a very strong, indirect factor.

Cathy McCoy-Morgan: It was very sad losing John Kennedy but I didn't think that had anything—I don't know if that set the mood. I was already in the mood for something new musically because it was boring. And I like music, and I like to dance, and I was waiting. And they did it.

Pete Kennedy: There was a vacuum that was waiting to be filled. You had all these baby boomers with all the energy of adolescence. But more than that, it was a generational desire to establish ourselves as being different, to establish ownership over our own generation and what our values were going to be, what we were going to be like, and how we were going be different from the 1950s people before us. And the Beatles personified all of that right at the same time.

* * *

What is still remarkable today is the astounding speed at which this original groundswell of interest in the Beatles accelerated into a genuine fanaticism. For the record, it all took a grand total of six weeks to happen—from the release of "I Want to Hold Your Hand" on December 26th, to their appearance on *The Ed Sullivan Show* on February 9th.

Here's a brief and simplified timeline to demonstrate just how quickly Beatlemania took hold:

Let's go back a few weeks before "I Want to Hold Your Hand" was released, to December 4, 1963. On this day, Capitol Records acquired all U.S. rights to Beatles songs (after having rejected them four times before) which, in theory, would put an end to seeing Beatles songs appearing haphazardly, and without publicity, on a number of small, independent labels. Thus began the long albeit imperfect association between the Beatles and Capitol Records (the group released their music in Britain on the Parlaphone label owned by EMI until they formed their Apple label in 1968). Right from the get-go, Capitol notoriously cannibalized the Beatles' British LP releases, taking out songs from this album and that, throwing 45 singles into the mix, and miraculously creating even more Beatles LPs than the Beatles themselves released in their native land (more about that later). For better or worse, Capitol now had the Beatles' songs to promote and sell here, and with the resources to do so vigorously.

Then there were the radio DJs, and their indispensable contribution to the story. By the early 1960s, radio as a vibrant medium for dramas and comedy programs had already died, thanks to the earth-shaking effect television had on American popular culture a decade earlier. However, radio enjoyed a new lease on life as it became the lifeline between American teenagers and the perpetual onslaught of new singers and groups who relied on that young audience to make or break their careers. Disc jockeys almost become like members of the family ("Cousin Brucie" couldn't have been a more apt nickname for New York DJ Bruce Morrow) to whom teenagers turned to hear the latest new song or artist.

Transistor radios became virtual appendages to teenage bodies, and were often smuggled into junior high school classrooms, only to be confiscated by disapproving teachers. Alas, those teachers and principals across the country would soon find themselves on the losing end of a battle of wills against Beatle-addicted students. In the last days of 1963, the airwaves were becoming increasingly crowded with new Beatles songs, with each song generating greater interest than the one before.

* * *

Pete Kennedy: I think transistor radios had a huge impact on the whole thing . . . suddenly we were in control of the radio. It wasn't the big family radio in the wooden cabinet, it was our own little thing that we carried around with that earphone. You could be glued to the radio almost all the time. So we got a much bigger dose of music than the kids before—as much as they loved Elvis, they didn't have as much opportunity to be absorbed in the music.

* * *

Radio provided the catalyst for Beatlemania, as DJs across the country both created and subsequently responded to the increasing demand to play more and more Beatles songs. Even so, the group hadn't had a true hit as of mid-December.

That all changed on December 17th when the first and probably most important breakthrough of all occurred for the Beatles, courtesy of disk jockey Carroll James at WWDC in Washington, D.C. On that day, James, who had obtained the British 45 of "I Want to Hold Your Hand," played it for the first time on American airwaves. For his young listeners, hearing that song was a life-changing moment. And soon other stations across the country picked up on the song and played it to their own audiences, receiving the same reaction. In fact, due to its early and almost constant radio airplay, listener demand prompted Capitol to release the single four weeks ahead of schedule, on the day after Christmas—December 26, 1963. Consequently, "I Want to Hold Your Hand" became the song most of the original fans remember as *the* song igniting Beatlemania.

* * *

Barbara Boggiano: At that time, for music, we had the Beach Boys, Elvis Presley, the Everly Brothers, "Teen Angel" type of stuff, people dying in car crashes, "Leader of the Pack," with this death and destruction. And into all of this is this band from England, and it was so exciting to hear something else. I was listening to 1010 WINS in New York. Murray the K had his show—of course at that time there was Cousin Brucie, but my sister and I mostly listened to Murray the K. He was saying the Beatles were this hot new band, they had just come back from Hamburg, they're sensational. Just listening to "I Want to Hold Your Hand" my sister and I were both looking at each other saying, "This is so original!" It just went from there. The station played various cuts from their album, and of course at that point you're going to school and talking with all your girlfriends, "Did you hear this?"

Mary Ann Collins: The first thing I ever became aware of was when the local radio station started talking about this new group, this new unusual group from England who had this song that was becoming a big hit called "I Want to Hold Your Hand." The first time I ever heard that song, I just thought it was fabulous, and was so different. So I became aware that the group that had made this song was called the Beatles.

Maryanne Laffin: I know exactly where I was and what song came on the radio when I first heard them. I was on the kitchen floor cleaning out a cabinet and "I Want to Hold Your Hand" came on the radio. That was it! It was just electric. I was eleven. And I look at eleven-year-old girls today and it's like, wow, they don't know what they're missing!

Cathy McCoy-Morgan: Then there was "I Want to Hold Your Hand" and it was just instantaneous. It was something so fresh and new, and really great.

Carol Moore: Back then, every week WABC would have the "Pick Hit of the Week." We were all very much into listening to the radio, and had been for a few years, so we were very aware of bands coming up. We heard talk about the Beatles, and there were the fan magazines, but it was just something that was coming, but whether or not we should be excited about it, we didn't really know. And then they had the Pick Hit of the Week, and this was the first time we had ever heard "I Want to Hold Your Hand." And it was just mind-blowing. It was a totally new style of music, totally exciting. I had been a bit of a skeptic myself, but as soon as I heard it, I of course realized what was going on.

Linda Cooper: I lived in the Maryland–D.C. area and used to listen to Carol James on WWDC. And then they started playing "I Want to Hold Your Hand," and then of course we kept hearing about the Beatles. I think the next record I got was "She Loves You." I can't remember when *Meet the Beatles* came out, when I first got that. I listened to "Till There Was You," and there was nobody else but McCartney in my book. That was it for me!

My mother gave me 35 cents a day for lunch money. And I ate an ice cream sandwich for a dime and kept the rest so I could save up for albums.

Betty Taucher: I first heard the Beatles soon after Christmas, the beginning of '64, in January. "I Want to Hold Your Hand." It was a Valentine's present from my mother, in my lunchbox. And I still have it. I have all my records still—all mono, cause I only had my record player.

You were just excited by the sound, 'cause I wasn't that into music before then. I was in seventh grade and I can't remember anything in particular that I listened to before that. You heard songs, like "My Boyfriend's Back"—nobody was into that, and none of us were into Elvis, so when that song hit it was just a totally different sound. We had no clue what they looked like, 'cause we heard the song first on the radio, on KYW. That was when you listened to the radio for a particular DJ.

Paula Lewis: I grew up in a very small town in north Texas, almost in Oklahoma. It's about 75 miles from Dallas. I could pick up the Dallas radio stations during the daytime. I do remember when I heard "I Want to Hold Your Hand" it was like nothing I had heard before. And it really got my attention.

Maggie Welch: I played sick from school on the 2nd of January, 1964. Up until this time, I had never really heard rock & roll music playing. My family played only classical music. I played violin, viola, and clarinet, and I just happened to turn on the radio—I'd been hearing a little Beatles, of course, from my friends, being over at their houses, and started to get curious about it. So I heard this song, but the title "I Want to Hold Your Hand"—give me a break. But then the DJ said, "There's that song from the English group." And I've been an Anglophile for as long as I can remember. Well, maybe I'll give it a second listen. And the rest is history. I gave it a second listen and said, "Hey, this is really something new and different, and has the potential of being extremely exciting."

* * *

Two weeks after the release of "I Want to Hold Your Hand," Vee-Jay Records defiantly released the album *Introducing the Beatles* on January 10th, 1964, prompting a series of complex lawsuits and counter-suits between Vee-Jay and Capitol. Fans were oblivious to such legal wrangling. Their take on it was simple: the more Beatles songs they could hear, regardless of who released the records, the better.

On January 18th, "I Want to Hold Your Hand" entered Billboard's Top 100 chart at #45. Two days later, Capitol released the *Meet the Beatles* album, which was to sell 3 ½ million copies in the next two months.

* * *

Paula Myers: When "I Want to Hold Your Hand" and "She Loves You" came out, we were hooked. I remember going to a store near where we lived, and our joy there was the *Meet the Beatles* album on display. We loved their long hair. They looked so cute and very similar on the cover photo of the album. I think we bought the album that day. This was the beginning of a long love affair with the Beatles, Paul in particular. Paul was our favorite.

Deborah McDermott: I think I was 12 when *Meet the Beatles* came out, but I have a very distinct memory of being in a grocery store with my mother, and seeing the album and begging her to get it for me. Even at 12 years old it was the talk among us. It was in Washington, D.C., in a giant grocery store, and I remember the moment. I can see my mother, and I can see me, in this record aisle, and she kind of rolled her eyes and got it. And you'd heard all the songs on the radio, you'd heard "I Want to Hold Your Hand" particularly, and "I Saw Her Standing There," and it was a transporting event.

* * *

There was Beatles hype created by the record executives, concert promoters, and radio stations, to be sure, but more significantly, there was old-fashioned word-of-mouth. And, with unstoppable momentum, out of the mouths of babes in the days bridging the end of 1963 and beginning of '64 came the words, "You gotta hear this!"

JoAnne McCormack grew up in Queens as another early fan, becoming enthralled with the Fab Four in December of '63.

* * *

JoAnne McCormack: My girlfriend said, "There's this new group called the Beatles, and they sound pretty good." We went down her basement, and she played "I Saw Her Standing There" and "I Want to Hold Your Hand" and that was IT! I was gone. So that was the beginning.

All I wanted for Christmas was a record player because that's when I first got into the Beatles. So my parents bought me one with the plastic casing and the little turntable—at that time it was 30 dollars. That was the best thing anybody could have given me!

Leslie Barratt: It was 1963, and I remember my older sister, who is two and a half years older than me, mentioning some group and looking at pictures of these long-haired singers. And at the time, since we lived so close to New York City, we were always interested in various groups that were coming to town, or were in town. We kept up with that and listened to the radio—Murray the K, Cousin Brucie—and it was a picture in a magazine that she had seen. At some point, either in '63 or right at the beginning of '64, she said this group—I don't even know if I knew them as the Beatles—was coming to New York. And so we began to get really excited. I went into New York sometime before they came, and I went to a music shop in Rockefeller Center that specialized in singles from other countries, and I went in to buy a Beatles single—either "Please Please Me" or "She Loves You." And the flip side was "Love Me Do." So that one turned me on.

Brian Tourville: My band had been playing Beach Boys music up until that time. I was listening to WBZ Radio 103 and "She Loves You" came on. I was blown away by the pace of the energy and the harmonies. Immediately I called my lead guitarist to ask if he knew anything. He had heard "I Want to Hold Your Hand" but not "She Loves You." And that started everything from there on out, including school skits and Beatle wigs!

Douglas Edwards: Having a family that liked music was an influence in itself. My parents both used their stereo a lot. I had an older brother who was a teenager in the early '60s, so he listened to Elvis and the doo-wop music of that era.

With local television in those days having only a few channels and not a lot of programs, music was an enjoyable way to pass the time. I first became aware of the Beatles while listening to AM radio from Cleveland. Being 53 miles south of Cleveland, there were two 50,000-watt rock and roll stations that were easily listened to. Also, there was an AM station in Akron, WHLO; while not as powerful, it was only 20 miles away and played all the latest rock & roll. At night while in bed I used to hide my transistor radio under my pillow and listen to music or sports. The first 45 I bought was "She Loves You" on the Swan label. Their sound was different, but good different, if you know what I mean.

Wendi Tisland: I grew up in northern Minnesota, in a town of about a hundred in population. And I think at night only we got KDWB and WDGY, and that's where I first heard the Beatles. I don't particularly remember a song, but I knew as soon as I heard them I was a fan—the number one fan in northern Minnesota!

Art Murray: I was listening to the car radio consistently during that era, as I think most kids did, at least most kids where I lived which was northern Jersey rock radio, WABC, WMCA, WOR, all those stations, that's where you heard music. And I had been listening to Buddy Holly, Elvis, and the girl bands of the early '60s—Phil Spector's stuff, the Shirelles—I knew a lot of good music as I think most kids did. Not in a scholarly way, just listening to a tune and liking it. But I fancied myself more of a jazz fan. That was the era of the Playboy influence, and the idea of being suave and Bond-like, and that was in jazz. So I wanted to be cool. And rock was fun, but jazz was cool. So I thought of myself as being attracted to Dave Brubeck's "Take Five," etc.

The Beatles came up, and the first tunes I heard were "I Want to Hold Your Hand" and "She Loves You," which were both huge hits, and they were all over the radio. And they were wonderful, but my sister, who was four or five years younger, was the one who was listening to them, I wasn't. I was listening, but I didn't like them, or *thought* I didn't. The music was wonderful, I knew that, but they were the Beatles. They were oddballs. I was too cool for the Beatles. They were for girls to shriek about. They were to be looked at askance by guys! If you were cool, you didn't like the Beatles. Now this attitude of mine lasted maybe 20 minutes, but it was long enough that I remember.

Debbie Levitt: I heard "Love Me Do" first, but my favorite is "She Loves You." There's something about the vocals on that song that just gets to me where I get the chills! There isn't a bad one in the bunch, but maybe it's that one that does it to me. The early stuff had to evolve into the later stuff, and to me it's not "bubblegum" and not pop—it's what it was at the time.

Janet Lessard: When I first started hearing about the Beatles it was February of '64, so I was barely 14—I was actually 13 and a half. There was nothing else occupying my thoughts. You have to realize that I don't think girls were as mature at 13 and 14 and 15 in the '60s as they certainly are today. Boys hadn't really entered the picture at that point. And it was almost like, here come these four guys that were so different, and had such a different sound, and it was almost like having a first love. There was nothing else to distract us from this—the group of friends that I had. It was just like the most important thing in our life at that point.

Valerie Volponi: I think what we liked most about them was that there were four of them, they played their own instruments, and they wrote their own songs, which was a lot different than the groups before them. No other groups were writing and recording their own songs, so they were very unique. There hadn't been a singing group here from any other country before. England suddenly became popular, and we wanted to know everything about England and London. We got a hold of magazines from England—one of them was called *Rave*, and there was *Beatles Monthly*. I was in high school at the time and had four very close friends, and all of us spent every waking minute talking about them. It really consumed a lot of our time.

Linda Cooper: The music just kind of caught me—it was exciting, and it was romantic, as much as I understood at the time. Years later I was thinking, well now I know why everybody was screaming, it was all of this sexual energy, but at the time I was stupid or naïve, or too young to understand what the heck was going on. And they were so personable and so fun. They just were so different.

* * *

Even those who don't claim to be Beatles scholars most likely remember *The Ed Sullivan Show* as being the first American program on which the group performed. This is true, in a way. Yes, it was the first program on which they were invited to perform live for an American television audience, and that would occur on February 9, 1964. However, it was actually on January 4th when American TV viewers—at least those who watched Jack Paar—caught their first brief glimpse of the group via a film clip. Paar had cemented his reputation as a quick-witted TV host during his five-year reign as host of *The Tonight Show* from 1957–62. It was during his subsequent prime time show when an amused and somewhat perplexed Paar offered a few comments as he aired a portion of the Beatles singing "She Loves You."

* * *

Linda Cooper: My parents used to watch Jack Paar, and I remember they had a little blurb about them on. And I saw them and thought, who are these guys? 'Cause they had the collar-less suits on, and they were doing "She Loves You." And I thought, "Wow, this is really interesting!" My parents thought it was pretty funny, they thought [the Beatles] were really odd-looking and all that. And I remember feeling so offended, and that's when I called my girlfriend Sharon and said, "You should see what I just saw!"

Barbara Allen: It was a Friday evening. *The Jack Paar Show.* I would have been in ninth grade.

I was at home with my parents (and two younger sisters), and usually on Friday nights we would put that on, because that was considered real entertainment in those days. And they usually watched the TV with us. And it was a little more sophisticated than the average TV show. It was really wonderful because on that night, he presented something that he said he wanted us to see. He said, "I have something here that I filmed recently in England, and I was so overwhelmed by this, I brought it back with me and I want you to see it." And that was the Beatles. He had a film in those days of a concert that they had put on somewhere in England, and he was so taken back by the reaction of the girls, that he had to bring that over and present it. And that would have been my first exposure to the group.

He always had that dry sense of humor, a little bit sarcastic. In that vein he was like, "Can you believe this?" It also, I think, fascinated him in a way, that he was perhaps surprised by. And you could hardly hear the music, but they were so unusual looking because they had these little suits on and they had their long hair—and that in itself was unique.

I was fixated by this. I couldn't believe my luck that I happened to watch this that night, because nobody had heard a thing about them. But that night I remember telling a friend about this. It just started this incredible curiosity, which started to be promoted by radio stations. Within another month, all of this promotion was being done, "The Beatles Are Coming to America." And since I had already seen the film clip, I was really mesmerized by them. I couldn't wait to see these guys on TV. They're gonna be on *Ed Sullivan*. There was this incredible hype and build up for that, and what happened was, all the girls started to get really crazy, even before they came to the country on that Pan Am jet. People were just so hyped up, even before they set foot on the soil. So this was something we could covet as our very own.

Cathy McCoy-Morgan: I saw them on *The Jack Paar Show* when I was about 13 years old. And I really didn't understand what the hubbub was . . . it was a little film clip about them, and they really didn't play their music, it was just about the mania that was happening and these women and girls and kids that were following them. And I thought, "Wow, that's kind of different." I didn't know why, or what was going on.

June Harvey: I think the first time I saw them was on *The Jack Paar Show*. He was more talking about their hair than anything else. Soon after that their music was being played on the radio stations. I just liked their sound. We had grown up with Motown and all of that, and this was definitely different.

Pete Kennedy: It seemed to me, having grown up in the '50s, that suddenly everything before that was a black & white movie, and suddenly the Beatles were like CinemaScope.

Art Murray: I can remember my sister upstairs in the spare room blasting those tunes, and listening to them thinking it was great stuff, but it was "junk." And that was the way I thought of it. Also, the Beatles had long hair—and long hair then being hair that today being considered conservative—but it was enough of a look that had become identified with them, so there was a fashion thing running concurrently, and that again had absolutely no appeal for me. My idea was a golf sweater, hair combed down over your forehead coolly, and if you could afford a Corvette, you'd get one. I couldn't even come close—I couldn't afford the sweater, but I had the attitude about it. That was the way you were supposed to be.

Charles Pfeiffer: In late 1963, early 1964, my sister, who is four years older than me, was talking about Beatlemania and there was a local radio station in Kansas City, Missouri, called WHB. It was a Top 40 station, that started playing "I Want to Hold Your Hand" and "She Loves You," so I was just excited. I didn't know what they were, or what was going to be.

Janet Lessard: My group of friends didn't know about the Beatles until they first played that song, "I Want to Hold Your Hand." It came on I think in January, on one of the radio stations around here that we all listened to. And it was such a completely different sound, and again, you couldn't just go on the computer and find out about this group or turn on the news. We were restricted to either listening to the radio or buying fan magazines, and we got a look at these guys and started reading more about them, and it just kind of caught on. It was just a phenomenon. And it wasn't just the girls. I can remember even the boys in our class were infatuated with them, in a different way, of course. They adopted the haircuts, the dress, and so on, and they loved the music too. And it was just such a new sound. Everything was so new, between the British accents and a different beat, and different lyrics, especially. It was the lyrics I think everyone caught on to.

When Elvis Presley first came on the scene, that was so different that it caught everyone by surprise, and there had been nothing different for another ten years when the Beatles came onto the scene. It was so different from anything that was out there, it just attracted so many people.

The radio stations must have realized they had a good thing because they would cash in on this. Every week they would play another song that had been #1 in England, and the next week another song, so it was just one song after the other, and everybody was just caught up in this.

Cathy McCoy-Morgan: By February of '64, everybody was talking about the Beatles, and the music was being played here. When I was a kid I'd come home from school and instead of watching kid shows I'd put *American Bandstand* on. And I just always loved music. But I got to the point where, I don't know, just—I was waiting for something. Nothing was going on. It was crappy music like Paul Anka. Then the Beatles came and it was something so new, and so fresh and so wonderful. Everything changed. The hairstyles, the clothing, everything was more free.

And I'll always remember this one woman who was interviewed, and she said how they're playing for everyone but it just feels so personal. It really was just incredible. It was a wonderful time.

* * *

By this point, with Beatlemania growing in intensity by the day, radio was becoming more instrumental than ever in contributing to the excitement.

* * *

Barbara Allen: And, of course, we had the radio on all the time because there were stations out of New York that played this music all the time: Cousin Brucie,

Murray the K, and they were playing the music and they'd always say, "Oh, we talked to Ringo on the phone last week . . . " or "I just got a letter from Paul" and they would try to fuel the flames, because the girls wanted to know everything. You couldn't hear enough about them. You wanted to know about their girlfriends, and where they went on vacation, and the music, and anything about them. And these guys kept the hype going.

Claire Krusch: The song "I Want to Hold Your Hand" was already number one, and that's all you heard. You never heard any other Beatles song for maybe a month, on WABC. WABC renamed itself "WABeatleC."

Paul Chasman: When they came to the U.S. the radio stations were doing a big deal about the countdown to when they were going to land in the U.S. I think I was home sick at that time, listening to all that hype, Casey Kasem and all that.

Valerie Volponi: We listened to the radio every night, and listened to Murray the K. He would always have interesting stories about the Beatles. So he was very exciting to listen to, with the new songs coming out.

Penny Wagner: I begged for a little transistor radio that year, and got it for Christmas. It was the cool thing to do, holding it and carrying the earpiece in your ear and dancing to the music while you're on the street walking. WOKY played them, I remember Bob Berry was instrumental in me listening to the Beatles. We used to call in with all these requests for certain Beatles songs, and they used to say they can't play it any more, it's been played non-stop. And every time somebody would call the radio station they'd be screaming in his ear, carrying on over the music.

Mary Ann Collins: At night, if you were careful with the tuner on your radio, we could get really far away stations like WGN in Chicago, and sometimes even WABC up in New York. I can remember one time there was going to be a release of a new Beatles single. And I didn't have any luck—I don't know if it's the way my house was positioned on the lot, or the way my girlfriend's house was closer to the water or whatever, but her reception on her radio was a lot better than mine. She could get the far away stations better than I could. So on this one particular night, when this one station far away was going to premiere "I'll Be Back," at the appointed time, I called her on the phone. And the two of us are on the phone, she's got the phone up to the radio, and I'm listening to this song over the telephone. That's the kind of stuff we did. And we just had the time of our lives with all that.

CHAPTER TWO

The First Invasion

Even with their astounding success in Britain and Europe, the Beatles were adamant about going to America only after they first had a #1 record in the States. They had seen other British pop singers try to make a name for themselves here without first securing a #1 hit, only to be placed third or fourth on concert bills, resulting in lackluster support from American audiences and record buyers. Brian Epstein needed to stay ahead of the curve. He had booked the Beatles on *The Ed Sullivan Show* back in November, getting them top billing for their three appearances. He also told promoter Sid Bernstein, who wanted to book them into Carnegie Hall, that the group would have to receive heavy radio airplay first. In fact, the idea of touring America at all as a top-of-the-bill act was, in Epstein's mind, contingent on the kind of substantial airplay and exposure they would receive in the weeks leading up to the *Sullivan* show.

The waiting ended when the January 25th issue of *Cash Box* magazine placed "I Want to Hold Your Hand" in the #1 spot, giving it the honor of becoming the first Beatles single to do so in America. By February 1st, the song reached #1 on the more prestigious *Billboard* chart as well. It was everything the Beatles had been hoping for.

The stage was now set. The final bookings were made. The invasion of America was next.

With their much-anticipated appearance on *The Ed Sullivan Show* fast approaching, the accompanying hype and building excitement would continue to increase until reaching critical mass.

* * *

Leslie Barratt: Every week Ed Sullivan always announced who was going to be on next week's show. But we knew definitely before that. We had enough time to get super-excited, and not enough time that we'd be waiting and waiting forever.

And so then, closer to their visit, we got more and more excited, and we were definitely listening and buying the magazines about them. I joined a Beatles fan club, and had several friends in junior high school who were getting very excited by the Beatles. Our middle school was right near downtown Hillsdale, New Jersey. And we were allowed to go downtown for lunch. So instead of going downtown and eating, which is what most of the students did, we went downtown and into the shop at least several times a week to see if they had any new magazines, and we knew what days of the week they'd come out, and we'd go in and buy the magazine and pore over it at lunch. So by the time the Beatles got there, we were a couple of months into Beatlemania, at least.

Barbara Boggiano: And *16* magazine at the time was *the* magazine. So as soon as I got my allowance, I was buying the latest edition. There was an article in *16* magazine, and it said would you like a Liverpool pen pal. They had hooked me up with a girl named Elizabeth from Liverpool, and a lot of my friends had gotten pen pals. That was exciting because I could actually write to someone who had been in the Cavern. All I could do was look at pictures, but she could write to me and tell me about just being down there, and experiencing that. And that to me was just fabulous.

Penny Wagner: Even though I was not 16 at the time, there was a magazine called *16*, and my older cousin, who was 16 at the time, always got it, and when she came over she always gave me the magazines. So that's when I first saw the Beatles. And then I heard they were going to be on *The Ed Sullivan Show*—and I come from very strict Catholics—and I begged my mom if we could watch *Ed Sullivan* that night, to see the Beatles.

Paula Lewis: Once I realized they were going to be on *Ed Sullivan* on my birthday, it was just too exciting. My parents were not happy about it. The long hair was really a big issue. The norm was the crewcut. It was especially disturbing to my father. All I wanted for my birthday was their newest album. I did get it, but my dad was really not happy about the whole idea of the long hair and this radical stuff.

Harold Montgomery: I went to school on the Friday before *The Ed Sullivan Show*, and *every single person* on the bus—I have to admit it was mostly the girls, but everybody had the 45 of "I Want to Hold Your Hand." It was like *the* thing to walk around carrying that single. It was amazing.

* * *

On Friday, February 7th, one week after "I Want to Hold Your Hand" became the Beatles' first #1 hit in America, the Beatles arrived in New York's newly named John F. Kennedy International Airport at 1:20 P.M., aboard Pan Am flight 101, to the welcome of 3,000 screaming fans. With their first step off the portable stairway ramp from the plane, the Fab Four secured their foothold for their invasion of North America.

* * *

Claire Krusch: I was in sixth grade when the Beatles came in, on a Friday afternoon—you don't forget these things. It was sunny out, it was cold, and the principal of my grammar school came into the classroom and said, "If anyone has a transistor radio, and they're going to listen to this group that's coming to

JFK airport, to hear when they're coming in. . . . " I thought he was going to say we could listen to it, and I got real excited. He said, ". . . I will take them away." And he made the announcement to our teacher so we could all hear it. He had problems with people sneaking in radios knowing that this group was going to be coming to the United States that afternoon.

Debbie Levitt: When I got wind of it that they were coming here and it was supposed to be a big blitz, I figured, "Oh, Debbie has to go to the airport!" And I told my friends about it because they started to play the records, and nobody was interested. "It's too noisy, it's too loud, it doesn't make any sense, what are you doing wasting your time? . . . " I know it's gonna go big and it's gonna go far. I had my mother write a note, "My daughter has something important to do, she won't be in."

Annette Joseph Walker: I decided that's where I wanted to go, so I called a friend of mine, and we headed off to the airport. I remember the subways being very crowded, so I'm sure it was morning rush hour. We got out there, and it was girls just everywhere. I remember just standing around, and these girls came over and asked if we had any information as to where they would be coming in, so we kind of banded together, about six of us, and we found out where the plane was coming in.

We stood at the observation deck, where you could actually look out onto the tarmac, to try to figure out where this plane was going to land. And then we found a hangar, and we climbed on top of this hangar. There was a ladder on the side of the building that went straight up, and we climbed up on the building, which we later found out was a UPS holding facility for their small planes. And we were up there for the longest time, and saw planes coming and going, but it never dawned on us that they would actually be coming down the steps from a plane, because back then they didn't have those ramps that push up to the plane door. We never did see anything. The security guards finally spotted us up there and forced us to come down.

Shaun Weiss: It's like it happened yesterday, so it's pretty vivid in my mind. My mom and dad were flying home into Kennedy Airport from the Caribbean. My elder sister and I had to go and pick them up. After we got there, we ran into hordes of girls. And, living in New York City at the time, some of the girls we knew. When we ran into a bunch of friends of ours, we asked them, "What are you guys doing here?" The tops of the buildings were covered with the fans. And they said, "We're here for the Beatles." And my sister and I said, "Who the hell are the Beatles?" These girls had photographs, a lot of them had signs . . . My dad took photographs from the plane window looking at the fans standing on top of the building. And he joked to my mom saying, "Look, all those girls are there for me!"

* * *

The Beatles immediately made their way to the Pan Am lounge for a prearranged press conference. They were followed by a swarm of fans, reporters, film crews, and casual observers who found themselves swept up in the commotion.

A blurry but fascinating shot of the crowd awaiting the Beatles' arrival at JFK airport, taken by Nat Weiss as his plane taxied in moments earlier.

* * *

Annette Joseph Walker: We went through the terminal, and you could see a whole stampede just heading in this one direction. We got down there right as they were passing by. We were back about 20 people deep, and you could only see the tops of people's heads, but we thought we had just gone to heaven!

* * *

Once at the Pan Am lounge, adorned with the airline's familiar logo serving as a backdrop, the Beatles stood on a platform in front of an array of microphones. They patiently waited for the photographers to settle down, but cries of "down in front!" and "give me some room!" threatened to stall the proceedings indefinitely. Press agent Brian Somerville asked for quiet, but when this was met with even more grumbling, he grabbed a microphone and demanded, "All right, shut up! Just shut up!" The Beatles jokingly repeated the admonishment, and the press conference finally got under way.

From that moment on, the Beatles quickly and easily charmed the army of reporters, who shouted out a steady barrage of questions and received a high quotient of clever one-liners in return ("Will you sing for us now?" "No, we need money first." "When will you get a haircut?" "I had one yesterday.") As first impressions go, the Beatles couldn't have created a better one. The group then made their escape from the airport to their new home away from home, the Plaza Hotel on 5th Avenue.

* * *

Annette Joseph Walker: I've been to the airport since, and I've never been able to imagine what was there that day. I didn't see anyone that looked like they were actually there to catch a flight. It looked like it was just Beatles fans. At that point it wasn't an airport, there weren't people milling around—everybody that was in the way got out of the way. It was chaos, and the decibel level—the planes landing were nothing compared to the roar in this place. It was like a steady hum, but it was just people screaming. And we went right from the airport to the Plaza.

Shaun Weiss: The girls told us they were going back to the Plaza Hotel, where the Beatles were staying. My sister and I decided we needed to investigate more about who these four guys were. But we got caught up in the hysteria of it. So we dropped my mom and dad off at home and we went on to the Plaza Hotel. We turned on the radio and heard Murray the K, standing out there with hundreds of girls, and very few boys.

* * *

It was no secret that the Beatles and their small entourage had booked a suite of rooms on the 12th floor of the Plaza Hotel for their stay in New York. The 3,000 fans who welcomed them at JFK Airport would prove to be merely the first throng of screaming teenage girls to greet them at their scheduled stops in Manhattan and beyond. The scene would repeat itself at concert venues, hotels, airports, and train stations throughout the Beatles' tour of the U.S. and Canada later in the year.

The steadily building crowd outside the Plaza kept track of the Beatles' whereabouts thanks to New York DJs such as Murray the K on WINS, and Cousin Brucie on WABC, who gleefully reported on the Beatles' progress through the city. Young filmmakers Albert and

David Maysles, hired at the last minute with a phone call from Granada TV in England, found themselves shoulder-to-shoulder with the group for the duration of their stay. They would capture each day of the group's visit on film—not just their public appearances, but also (and more interestingly) their more private moments in their hotel suites and while traveling from one destination to the next.

* * *

Leslie Barratt: I went into the city with at least one other friend. We often went into the city. We were not that far, and I had gone into New York City from the time I was 10 by myself. I started taking my friends into the city, just to go shopping, or go to the Plaza hotel, pretending we were guests, sitting around the lobby. It wasn't an unfamiliar location for us.

We made up our minds that we were gonna go. And we went in, and the real question was where to stand. But the police had cordoned off the street. We figured the Beatles were going to the front door. So everyone was standing there, and it was obvious to us, being so naïve, of course that's where they were gonna drive up in their limousines to the front door, like all these other cars were doing. And every car that came, we were peeking and we'd scream, and it was some old guy or something—not a Beatle. It was a big crowd. It was a zoo. Every girl our age was excited by the Beatles coming, so we were expecting a big crowd. After we found out that they had gotten there—and I think we found that out not by anybody telling us there, but everyone was holding up transistor radios at various times, and there were a lot of rumors going around. And you'd see a group of people start to do something, and you'd have to go over and find out what they were doing.

At one point we found out they were already there, that they had gone in through a back entrance, which of course devastated everybody. Then the question became what floor were they on, could we see them through the windows. We found out they were on the twelfth floor, and every time a curtain moved anywhere on the twelfth floor, everybody was screaming. Nobody had thought to bring binoculars. And a few times we saw a curtain move and it set everybody off.

At one point, we tried to call their room from a phone booth. And it wasn't just us, it was us and 15 other girls, as many as you can cram into a phone booth. Of course, the hotel didn't connect anybody to anything. But we stayed there for quite a while, because it wasn't just the arriving that was exciting, it was the fact that they were actually in that building. We're looking at a building, and the Beatles were in it! It's sort of—it's a very odd thing. And that fever was definitely there through the day. I can't tell you how many hours we stayed there.

Annette Joseph Walker: When we got there, the streets down 5th Avenue were blocked off three blocks in either direction. And they already had barricades up, and for some reason then they decided just to contain us in that area right in front of the hotel. People were sitting all over the fountain and in the street. They were still waiting for them to arrive, because everybody was very subdued, and at that point everybody was looking for the limo pulling in. Sometime later in the day, two or three limos did pull in, and all hell broke loose. We had no idea if they were in it or not, but it happened to be the only limo pulling up to the Plaza at the time. We stood out there screaming people's names and people would look out the window and the whole crowd would erupt. We had no idea where they were in the hotel, or even if they were on that side of the building. As it turned out they were, and we did get a spotting the next afternoon, but they had been out of the hotel and at Central Park, and we never knew they had left.

The rest of my time there, it was just one sighting after another—over here, over there . . . I remember some guy coming downstairs with these little baggies that they sell marijuana in now, and he had these little squares of cloth in them. And he told us he worked in the laundry, and these were the sheets they had slept on, and he had cut them into little squares and was selling them for a dollar a piece. The guy just disappeared into a sea of these girls, and when he emerged, they had taken everything he had on him. They could have been anybody's sheets for all we knew, but we didn't care. He said it was theirs, and we believed him.

Shaun Weiss: I heard a lot of their music that weekend because it was being broadcast on "WABeatleC" night and day, 24 hours a day. A lot of the girls had little transistor radios, so you can hear the music blaring. Standing there was amazing, because anyone who came to the window with longish hair, people just started screaming. Or if somebody drove up in a cab, somebody would yell, "It's Ringo!" and people would go crazy. It was just being swept up in this hysteria.

Leslie Barratt: There was always the possibility that they might come out again. The fact that they'd just flown from Europe didn't mean anything to us, or that they might be tired and taking showers. There was a possibility that we might see them through the window, that they might wave.

Annette Joseph Walker: People were trampling each other, it was chaos. The news people were standing around and thought this was just bedlam at that point; cameramen were being knocked to the ground.

We stole maids' uniforms and rolled up our pants and tried to get into the service entrance. There was a car parked about halfway down the block, with the windows down. And it had these uniforms in the back, probably just somebody's laundry. We didn't know if they were coming right back or not, so we just swiped the uniforms—they had "The Plaza" on them, so we went around the corner and put them on. We went to the service entrance, and rang the buzzer, and somebody pushed the door open, and we started inside. As the last one of us was getting through the door, a security guard stepped in front of us and asked to see our employee I.D. We had to say we didn't have one. He said, "You don't have one, do you." We said no. "Where'd you get the uniforms from?" "Somebody gave them to us." He made us take them off.

We sat and watched all sorts of other things. There was a girl who had been in the crowd earlier, and she said she was going to rent a limo. And we're thinking, yeah, right. Two hours later she pulls up in this limo and she's dressed to the nines, in her graduation dress or something. And they wouldn't let her in.

There was a building being constructed next to the Plaza, and we actually rode up in the little construction elevator that they had, and we got up to a certain point, and the thing stopped. Some guy shows up screaming at us, and lowered us back down. At one point, we found an air shaft on the side of the building and contemplated crawling through this thing! Something about the little dark tunnel stopped us from crawling through. We had gone and bought screwdrivers and everything to take the cover off it.

Shaun Weiss: And I stood out there. And that weekend, my sister Joanne and I literally were totally transformed into Beatle fans. What happened was as the weekend progressed towards Sunday, we started to find out things about them like where they were going to be, what shows they were going to do, dress rehearsals. And I befriended someone at the time whose name was Mal Evans. He was walking out of the Plaza very late Saturday night, out the side entrance. My sister and I were heading home, 'cause it was getting late. I heard an English accent, I went up to him and I thought he was one of the Beatles. He said no, he was the road manager. He told us that the Beatles were going to be on *The Ed Sullivan Show.*

* * *

The Beatles managed to spend the morning of the next day, February 8th, in relative quiet. John, Paul, and Ringo avoided the mobs of fans awaiting them in front of the Plaza by using a side door, and took a stroll through Central Park (George was stuck in bed with a sore throat). Of course, their "stroll" was really for the benefit of the army of journalists and photographers covering their visit. The streetwise photographers didn't quite know what to do with the group at first, so they shouted out instructions for poses like "point to the sky!" and anything else that came to mind. Next, the Beatles headed for the CBS theatre on 53rd Street, the home of *The Ed Sullivan Show*, for rehearsals.

Sullivan had witnessed Beatlemania first-hand during a trip to England back in September, but hadn't seen or heard the group perform. He was nonetheless impressed with the passion they instilled in their British fans, and in November negotiated with Brian Epstein to have the group perform on three separate Sullivan shows beginning in early February. The group would be paid a total of $10,000 for two live appearances plus a taping of a third performance to be aired later in the year.

The next day, on Sunday afternoon, the group performed a full run-through of the songs they would play on the show that night. They did so in front of a full studio audience, who had the privilege of getting the scoop on the rest of the country by several hours. A different audience was later brought in for the live broadcast. When the program went on the air at 8:00 P.M., it was viewed by an estimated 73 million people—the largest audience for a television show ever to that date. It was only six weeks after Capitol Records officially released "I Want to Hold Your Hand."

And it was the night Beatlemania exploded.

* * *

June Harvey: My friend's father worked for an ad agency and it just so happened that he had tickets for *The Ed Sullivan Show* for that night. A client had given them to him. But he did not want them, so he gave them to us.

Two days before, they came into JFK, and there was quite a bit of fanfare and excitement. I think some of my friends tried to go out to the airport to meet them. I was working on a project for school and couldn't get off, but I knew we had the tickets. And at that time we thought they were just a passing fad. We had no inkling that they would be some part of music history. It was just so early in their recognition factor. This was February, and their music had only started playing six weeks before. There was some momentum building, but really not any that I thought was over the top, other than when they came into JFK, I remember seeing on the news that there were a lot of screaming fans that had come out there.

The day of the show, my friend and I went down on the subway—we lived in the Bronx—and we'd take the Lexington Avenue line down. We had the tickets, but I do not think they were assigned seats, I think they were just entry tickets into the theatre. We had to wait outside for quite a long time, well over an hour, and it was freezing cold. I do remember that! There were two girls standing right behind us who were British. We struck up a conversation with them. They were on winter holiday, and one of the girls' brothers went to school with John Lennon, and she knew John. They were from Liverpool, and we talked about their friendship with some of the Beatles, especially John.

It was very electric, it really was, like something exciting was about to happen.

Shaun Weiss: By Sunday I was hooked. Sunday was very interesting for us. My sister and I knew where *The Ed Sullivan Show* was so we walked down to the theatre with a bunch of friends of ours. As the day progressed, we were trying to find tickets to get in. My sister started to put on crocodile tears, and we had run into these two older people who were standing on line to go in. My sister said, "Do you have any extra tickets?" and they turned around and said, "We actually have tickets for friends of ours, and we don't know if they're showing up. But if they don't show up, you can have them." So my sister attached herself to them. The friends never did show up, and when it came to getting into the theatre, they only put a certain amount of kids up front. They stuck the rest of us up in the balcony. But it didn't matter. It was so amazing just to be there and see Ed Sullivan walk out on that stage. We were in the last row of the balcony, by the center aisle. My sister snuck down to the first row of the balcony with one of her friends.

* * *

The Beatles kicked off the show with their first set of three songs: "All My Loving," "Till There Was You," and "She Loves You." Later in the show, after performances by the cast of *Oliver!* (featuring future Monkee Davey Jones), impressionist Frank Gorshin, and other acts commonly seen on Sullivan's show, the host brought them back to sing "I Saw Her Standing There" and "I Want to Hold Your Hand."

* * *

Shaun Weiss: When they came out to perform, you really lost sight of them onstage. It was just looking around and seeing girls screaming, and girls crying. Being as far up as we were, we really didn't see them as well as you would on TV sitting in your living room. Being there was a whole different excitement. I was so caught up in this moment, the reality was just *being* there was the thrill. I don't even remember the songs that were being played, just that I could not believe these guys from Liverpool were performing, and I was seeing this live. The charm of seeing them for the first time in person, and not really understanding what was happening to me. I was getting caught up in a hysteria that I didn't understand. Everything else was fogged out.

The theatre had a way of locking you in, so that you couldn't get out to bother the Beatles leaving. But we just opened the exit door and we all flew out, and tried to get around to the side to see them leave, but obviously they had other ways of getting out that we knew nothing about.

The things I remember about them were just their mannerisms—and how much fun it looked like they were having. But it also looked like they were kind of scared. Just their mannerisms standing there, and Ringo up on the drum set playing and his head shaking. . . . That weekend, walking into it, I was unaware of what I was walking into. For the next five years of my life, I was obsessed with them. And the more I became obsessed with them, the more I geared my life to kind of hang in their corner.

June Harvey: We must have been fairly close up in line because we were ushered into the balcony and we ended up in the first row. And the Ed Sullivan Theatre was very small, and the balcony hung right over the stage. I think Letterman has taken out the balcony. I was second from the end, and a photographer came in after all of us were seated, and there were a lot of screaming fans directly behind me. We were so close to the photographer that he could not get an angle on us. He leaned in and shot up over us. So all the pictures in the fan magazines were the people sitting right behind us, including the two girls from Liverpool.

The screaming was constant, but I remember hearing them sing, there's no doubt about it. And we were literally hanging right over the stage so we could see them. It was a memorable experience.

* * *

While 728 audience members in the theatre experienced the Beatles singing to them in person, 73 million more were watching at home across the country. It quickly became an entertainment event famous for having not only generated unprecedented anticipation, but for surpassing even the highest of expectations.

The reverberations felt throughout millions of households across the country that Sunday evening were immediate. For most parents watching the Beatles' performance, it was in parts laughable, cacophonous, unseemly, or worse. For their children, however, it was nothing short of electrifying. By the time that single hour-long program began rolling its closing credits at 8:58 P.M. Eastern Standard Time, the Beatles had generated an emotional shock wave of such intensity that it instantly sent an entire generation of American teenagers into a state of sheer exhilaration. An overstatement, perhaps? Not according to those who experienced it and who can still recall that night in vivid detail, and with that same youthful passion.

* * *

Janet Lessard: By the time they were on *The Ed Sullivan Show*, that was just—I can't even compare it to anything right now. It was just fantastic. We were literally gathered in each other's homes. We would sit there from six o'clock waiting for that show to come on at eight, in groups of fives and tens. We were just amazed.

Charles Pfeiffer: On that Sunday night in February of '64 we gathered around the black and white Zenith, and when they came on *Ed Sullivan*, all I can remember is Ed saying, "Ladies and Gentlemen, here's the Beatles!," and gosh, when they struck that first chord it just sent something through me. And I was a 12- or 13-year-old boy with a crew cut, and I remember I turned around and said, "I'm growing my hair out." That was the first thing I was gonna do, which I started to do. And just the minute they started to play, I thought, "Gosh, this is what I want to do."

Penny Wagner: My dad didn't want anything to do with it. I don't think he was home that night, but my mom said all right—she was pretty open-minded, and we sat down, my youngest sister and myself. She never even liked the Beatles, to this day! No interest whatsoever.

I turned into a Beatlemaniac from the minute I saw them sing "She Loves You" and "I Want to Hold Your Hand." That was it. I couldn't stop myself. I started screaming and carrying on, and my mother didn't know what to do with it—my grandmother thought something was wrong with me. And I'm still, to this day, an avid Beatle fan. I picked a favorite immediately, and what's so cool about this story is I got to meet him in real life. It was Ringo Starr. He was my favorite Beatle, from the minute I saw him on *Ed Sullivan* till now.

Leslie Barratt: I took pictures of them on the TV. It was the first time I saw them performing. My sister and I were upstairs and I know my parents came to the TV and looked at it, probably my younger brother, too—not very interested with these two girls screaming at the TV. At that point I was just completely blown over and in love with every one of them, although my favorite was Paul.

Linda Cooper: My parents were giving me so much grief, I went to my girlfriend Sharon's house to watch it. And it was just—you'll probably think it's goofy but I never was one of the girls who screamed and all that, but I would just sit there and cry! And so her father would laugh at me all the time and handed me his handkerchief and said, "You're gonna need this." So by the time they finished at the end of the show, all that was left of the handkerchief was the border. I ate the whole thing watching them.

Maryanne Laffin: I cried. I remember just sitting there crying. I didn't know why.

Janet Lessard: The tears—we would watch them on *The Ed Sullivan Show* and we would just dissolve into tears. I can't describe it. It was something that just came over us. It was so new, and overwhelmed us, I guess. Girls growing up in the mid-'60s were much younger, figuratively and emotionally, than girls growing up now. Girls 13, 14, and 15 now have already done all of this by now. This all happens to them much earlier. To us, we weren't really into boys or anything like that. And all of a sudden these four guys come around with their charm, their music, their witty remarks, and it just kind of hit us like a ton of bricks!

Claire Krusch: My sister and I had a reel-to-reel tape recorder, and we taped it. So we have that on tape, but the sound is terrible. Just listening to that and us going "Oh my God, look at them!" and screaming. I remember my dad saying, "Their hair is too long, but they look very neat."

Dale Ford: I actually took pictures of the television. They came out pretty good! I just thought they were the greatest. It was one of those things where you just knew that there was something special about them. I loved music and rock & roll, whatever was going on at the time. The Beach Boys were okay, Elvis I liked but I wasn't a huge fan or anything. But there was just something about the Beatles you just kind of knew that this was really, really going to be big. I just knew it. And of course I was madly in love with Paul McCartney.

Carol Cox: I was like two inches from the screen, screaming. I was a screamer. We had a next-door neighbor and many years later she said to me, "We thought somebody was being murdered over there, we could hear you screaming for the Beatles. So we always knew when they were on!" I can't articulate it all these years later. There was something about them. They were fresh, they were new, there was just something really special and magical. I wish I could pinpoint it. I still get it now, to this day. When I see the *Sullivan* shows, it takes my breath away.

Betty Taucher: I sat with my girlfriends to watch them. We were feeling the TV and touching it and screaming. My father was laughing hysterically on the couch at us. I had to clean the TV after that. And TVs then had those tiny little green screens, and it was black and white of course, we didn't have a color TV. And I don't think *Sullivan* was in color then either. We were embracing the TV and touching them and screaming, the whole nine yards. And after it was done I remember we were just lying on the floor and it was like, "Oh my God, what was that?"

Barbara Allen: My mother was always an open-minded person, but my father just said, "Oh my God, this is awful. How can you watch this?" The fathers were always negative towards them. They didn't like the hair, they didn't understand the music, they didn't know what we were carrying on about, and they would all make a comment. And my father said, "I'll bet you a dollar to a doughnut, in about four years, you wouldn't walk across the street to see those goofs." Well, if they were outside right now, I'd walk outside to see them, and I'm 55 years old!

Douglas Edwards: I remember watching with excitement as they led off the show. Before they were through with "All My Loving," I was hooked. They had a charisma about them that was different than anything that I had ever seen or heard. By the end of the *Sullivan* show that night, this 11-year-old was counting my allowance to see how soon I could buy the next single.

Paul Chasman: I remember seeing them and being almost attracted and repelled at the same time; attracted because they were just so damn good and magnetic, and there was still part of me that was resistant, not being sure that I was recognizing the real thing. But I was really excited about them, and always wanting to hear more.

Harold Montgomery: Up until the *Sullivan* show, I wanted to be an archeologist. And all of a sudden, bam! All the archeology things came down and I started going to the neighbor's house asking for newspapers to clip out and I started clipping out and saving everything that I ever found on them. It totally turned me completely around.

Kathy Albinder: The first time I saw them on *Ed Sullivan*, I can remember coming back from a family trip and pushing my father because we were gonna be late. I'm the oldest of eight kids, so I was there saying, "Come on, let's go, we're gonna be late!" So I think we missed the first half of it, but I did see the second half.

Paula Lewis: As I was watching it, I was remembering just a few years before when Elvis had been on, in 1956, and I have an aunt who is just a few years older than I am, and she was just so caught up with Elvis. And when he was on *The Ed Sullivan Show*, I was just six or seven, and she was screaming and crying, and just beside herself, and I was just not really caring what was on TV, but was fascinated with the way my aunt was carrying on. So when the Beatles were actually on, I was so enthralled with just seeing them, but afterwards I was thinking about how it was very much the way it had been for her. Some people couldn't watch it because it was Sunday night and they had to go to church. Those people were really outcasts in lots of ways. They really had missed an important thing.

Pete Kennedy: We were a little young for the liberation of Elvis. My sister was into him and the Everly Brothers, so I knew about them from watching *American Bandstand,* I knew about the Fifties rockers, but it wasn't specifically my music. And in '63 I liked Peter, Paul & Mary and the Kingston Trio, which also wasn't specifically my stuff, being 12 years old. And this was! It was this watershed—and the amazing thing to me is so many kids were experiencing the same thing all over the country at the same time, but we were all in separate houses on a Sunday night at eight o'clock. It was obvious to me these guys were breaking down that whole thing. I don't know if they had any intention of doing that, but that's what they did. It was a revolution, really.

Betty Taucher: The next day in school, that's all anybody talked about. And all of a sudden all of the boys that had their hair slicked back on Friday—on Monday, it was all combed down. Over the weekend it changed that much.

Shaun Weiss: After that Sunday night, my hair was pushed down—the next day in school, I didn't realize the historical event I was witnessing. I was just caught up in this Beatles moment.

Douglas Edwards: At school the next day, the Beatles were the only topic of conversation among the fifth graders at Watson Elementary. Before winter of '64 had thawed in northeast Ohio, I had every single the Beatles had released in that couple of months.

Dale Ford: I had an excellent childhood. I was one of these kids who I would come home from school, and my mom would have a pot of tea, and French fries and *American Bandstand* turned on the television—all waiting for me when I got home from school. This is the kind of life I had growing up.

I had a *wonderful* childhood. But, my dad said, "These Beatles aren't going to last, they're a flash in the pan, I've seen them come and I've seen them go. I don't know why you're getting all in an uproar over this. They're not gonna be around. . . . " Oh, I argued with him! He used to love to challenge me like that. He liked it when he pushed my buttons.

* * *

The day after the *Sullivan* show, the Beatles were to fly to Washington D.C. for their first American concert, at the Washington Coliseum. A snowy day required them to change travel plans and head for Penn Station. The train they took to Washington delayed its departure in order to add a private car for the group, their entourage, and the press.

Nine-year-old Linda Binns, of Richmond, Virginia, who was on a return trip from New York with her family, recognized the Beatles as they passed through her train car. She decided she wanted to join them. Her meeting was filmed and recorded by the Maysles brothers, who were traveling with the group and documenting their activities for the duration of their travels to D.C. and then Miami.

* * *

Linda Binns Liles: The reason my family was in New York was because my father got invited to be on the *I've Got a Secret* show. He was a judge, and when he was in high school, he had to stay after school one time and write 50 times on the blackboard "I must not talk during class." Thirty-eight years later, the teacher appeared in front of him in court. So he made her write 100 times, "I must not exceed the speed limit." It was one of those fillers that newspapers used, and was the thing that *I've Got A Secret* looked for. So they invited my dad and the teacher to be on the show, which was done live on Monday nights. We just happened to go up the weekend the Beatles first came to the United States. And we passed the Plaza, and the kids were screaming and yelling. And we went out to dinner Sunday night with my dad's friend, another lawyer he knew in New York, and we didn't even see the Beatles on TV. I'm one of the few people who didn't. Monday night my dad was on TV, and Tuesday we were taking the train back to Richmond, and it was snowing so hard the Beatles couldn't fly to their concert in D.C. So our train got delayed and they added a private car behind us. We were the last car on the train, and the only car with people that they actually went through and met. The next car they put the press in, then they locked the train. They knew once people knew the Beatles were on the train, they'd be trying to get back to them.

I'd heard some of their songs, but I wasn't really that big of a fan at that point in time because they were new. We didn't see them on *Ed Sullivan*, but I knew who they were, and we started to get their autographs, and I wanted to get all four autographs. They had gone off to do a press conference, and I only had two of the autographs at the time, so I decided that I wanted to go back to the press car. They weren't going to let me in at first, but then they decided, "She's just a kid," and they let me in. And I just went back there and sat with Ringo Starr for an hour, and just talked to him! For me, I guess the reason I was so calm about it was, I was thinking, okay, it's his first time in New York City, it's my first time to New York City, and he asked about my life. I was nine years old, and thought, of course he should be fascinated with *my* life. So I answered questions about my life, and talked to him about his. Just a great conversation, we laughed, and—I had told my dad where I was going, and he went looking for me, and found me—and the cameras were just flashing all the time—and he said, "You weren't paying any attention to it at all. You were just talking!" George Harrison was sitting across from Ringo and I the whole time, and we'd talk to him a little.

My brother and I were the only people who got invited to their private car. I had gotten everybody's autograph, and for some reason, maybe I knew in the back of my head they were famous, but I just felt that I had to kiss them on the cheek and thank them for their autograph. I'm from the South and you're always supposed to do something nice when people do nice things for you, so I decided I wanted to kiss them all on the cheek and say thank you, and they seemed to think that was just fine!

Ringo and I watched at every train stop—the word had come—and girls had gotten on the train, and jumping up and down on the platform trying to get a glimpse of them. And Ringo asked me, "Would you do that?" And I looked at him and said, "No, I would not do that!" And he thought it was funny, and we laughed and had a good time. Ringo asked me to marry him. But I turned him down because I had to get my education.

I went up to Paul and talked to him, and my brother said I asked Paul who writes their music! We just played around, and honestly, I knew who they were

Linda Binns Liles when she was a nine-year-old Linda Binns, chatting with Ringo aboard the train to Washington, D.C.

and I liked their music, but being in that moment, it didn't seem like it was something monumental. We were just having a conversation. Paul asked me if I was coming to the concert, and I said no, I had to go to school the next day. They had had so much attention, maybe it was nice for them to have someone talk to them and not be absolutely star-struck, and treating them like who they are.

I think that's one of the reasons that I actually got to spend the time I spent with them was because of the age I was. I was kind of under the radar for everybody.

* * *

The American broadcast of the Maysles documentary aired on CBS November 13, 1964.

* * *

Linda Binns Liles: On a Friday night, my parents had gone out and we were home, and one of my mother's friends called up and said, "I just saw Linda on TV with the Beatles!" And the Maysles brothers sold a version of their documentary to CBS, and Carol Burnett narrated a one-hour version of this. And I happened to be in a montage at the beginning. I actually have a 16 mm film of that. My father was a judge, and he wrote to CBS and said, "You didn't have permission to use my daughter's picture" and so he got them to send a copy, and he picked it up on Christmas Eve that year. And that was one of my Christmas presents. It was all set up, they had gotten a screen and projector. Of course we watched it then, and we put it away, and we pulled it out when I was in college and looked at it, and put it away. And I showed it about five or six years later and put it away, and haven't opened it since.

On the DVD, they have me on the train after the D.C. concert, even though I met them before that.

We came back to Richmond, and my father gave an interview for the Richmond paper, and then I can't tell you how many teenagers called our house to talk to me. I'd just get on the phone and tell them about it. They asked me every question imaginable. I would talk to them until my mother finally got tired of the phone being tied up, and then I couldn't talk to them anymore.

I have all four autographs on one sheet of paper, and so does my brother. I have two McCartney autographs. So, we had come back from New York and we had forgotten to buy our next-door neighbor a present, so I gave him Paul McCartney's autograph.

It was a wonderful experience, and it wasn't until I was older that I really realized that this was really a rare opportunity that not a lot of people actually got to do.

* * *

The Beatles' first U.S. concert, at the Washington Coliseum, took place on February 11th. There were several striking aspects of the performance. There was, of course, the sheer energy they generated singing their latest hits (including the spine-tingling three-part harmony on "This Boy," which they managed to maintain amid the chaos surrounding them). Perhaps most surprising in retrospect was the truly rudimentary nature of their concert presentation at the time. A bare stage stood in the center of the auditorium, surrounded by the seating on all sides, with a set of microphone stands for each side, and rather puny guitar amps. Ringo's drum set was set high on a small revolving stage—albeit one that needed to be turned by hand. Every few songs, Ringo—sometimes with assistance from another Beatle or a stagehand—would have to hop off and struggle to rotate the stage in order to face a new side of the crowd. John, Paul, and George, of course, merely stepped up to a different set of microphone stands. Still, the concert set the frenzied tone for all of the performances to follow on their U.S. tours (although the group already had much experience playing before the deafening screams of thousands of girls).

The next day, the Beatles took the train back to New York in order to perform at the prestigious Carnegie Hall. Concert promoter Sid Bernstein booked the hall for the first major rock concert ever to take place there.

The next stop on this whirlwind trip was Miami, Florida, where the Beatles performed for the second time in as many weeks on *The Ed Sullivan Show*, broadcasting from the Deauville Hotel. This trip to Miami actually afforded the group a few days of down time, giving them an opportunity to take in the sun before returning to New York for a quick stopover on their return flight back to England.

* * *

Pete Kennedy: I first heard of them the Monday morning *after* the first *Ed Sullivan* show—my twelfth birthday—so I never heard of them before *The Ed*

Sullivan Show, although I listened to the radio a lot. And the first DJ to play them, Carol James, broadcast in my area, Arlington, Virginia. But I didn't listen to his station, so I'd never heard the Beatles. And I went in to serve mass—I was an altar boy—and the other altar boys said, "Did you see the Beatles last night?" And at the time I was really into *The Flintstones* and *The Jetsons,* and I thought it was a cartoon show. And I said, "Is that a new show?" "No, no, man, it's a band, they were on *Ed Sullivan* last night!" But in the ensuing week, everything was, of course, the Beatles. So by the next Sunday, I tuned in to the Miami *Sullivan* show, and the following week. So within a week I was a hardcore Beatle fan, along with everyone else.

* * *

The Beatles' first visit to America had the impact of a tornado's sudden path of upheaval and its abrupt departure, leaving a permanently altered landscape in its wake. With barely a moment to look back on what they had just wrought in America, the group returned to the U.K. with a full schedule of concerts, television and radio appearances, interviews, and photo sessions waiting for them. In March, they even began filming their first feature film. Everyone wanted a piece of the Beatles, and the clamor for them just kept growing.

Back in the States, their fans were busy happily succumbing to the Fab Four's music and undeniable charisma, and were already counting the days until their return in the summer for their first big concert tour. The Beatles had become the front and center focus of young America's lives.

* * *

Betty Taucher: You wanted to talk like them, the boys all started to grow their hair like them—even though they weren't allowed long hair in school, they would comb their front hair down. You wanted to dress like them, everything.

Douglas Edwards: By the end of February '64, most of us were trying to talk with Liverpool accents, grow our hair and wear "Beatle boots" which were available at the local shoe stores. My dad had a thing about hair and he was not about to have his youngest son grow his hair "long." It's funny, looking back on it, how the adults thought the Beatles had long hair, when in reality, it wasn't very long at all.

David Rauh: I was one of the first to grow my hair long. I actually got kicked out of school for three days because my hair was too long. It was above my ears, above my collar in the back, but my bangs came to my eyebrows. So that was considered too risque, to have your bangs to your eyebrows, just like girls had to kneel down on the floor—if their skirt didn't touch the floor, they had to go home and change it 'cause it was too short! That's the way it was in the '60s.

Deborah McDermott: My father was at the time a manager of a Sears store in Washington, D.C., and there was a music department, and the record manager knew I was a Beatles nut, and he would always tell my dad the second a new album came in. And he'd hold a copy for me, and I was always the first kid on the block to get whatever the newest album was. And I became somebody people always turned to when they knew there was a new album coming out, because I would have it! It was kind of a cool place to be, 'cause I was always a step ahead of everybody else, by a few days.

Douglas Edwards: Almost every couple of weeks my dad would take me to the record store, which in those days was an extension of the local music store. I would buy one 45, so I had to choose well. My mom was a lot easier to talk into buying me a record when I went shopping with her. Sometimes she would even buy me two 45s! It was rare that I would get an album, but by summer I had *Meet the Beatles* and *The Beatles' Second Album*. I almost wore them out playing them constantly on the stereo. I would go into my room once in a while, put the 45s on my record player, grab a baseball bat and lip sync the words while using my Louisville Slugger as my guitar. Three of my neighborhood buddies and I bought some plastic guitars at Woolworth's. The guy who was going to be Ringo used an old hassock as his base drum and used some wood to make his snare and tom-tom. We called ourselves The Silver Satellites, and we lip synched the Beatles songs to the neighborhood girls in one of my friends' basements. We even signed autographs after our "concert" using the Beatles' names. The things you do when you're 11 years old!

David Rauh: For me it was not only the music, but fashion too. All the guys had to have Beatle boots, I had to have that leather cap that John had. And it continued on, 'cause I grew up with them. I remember when *Beatles VI* came out in the U.S. and George had that striped shirt with the white cuffs and the white collar. And I had to find one of those shirts!

Barbara Allen: When we were in school—this played out all over the place, not just at home, but in school—we'd be in class and people would pass these Beatles magazines all through the classroom. And after the guys were on *Sullivan*, *Life* magazine did an article that was great, that had all the photos of them in their hotel room at the Plaza. I know I have it in one of my scrapbooks. And we went berserk with that article because it had these really great photos in black and white of the four of them. And it went all through the classroom and the girls were kissing them, and you got them back and they had lipstick all over them. It was hilarious. This was so crazy.

Betty Taucher: My girlfriend brought her radio to school. You weren't *allowed* to have a radio in school. In those days they were much more strict about all that stuff. So she brought a radio and a rope—tied the radio on a rope and sat it on a ledge by the window. You couldn't hear anything anyway!

Maggie Welch: I had a big sign on my door that said "Quarantine—Beatlemania." And you'd walk in and there were just pictures all over the place. My family moved twice while I was still hanging things on my wall—now they're in frames—I had just scotch taped them on the walls. My poor parents had to have the painters sand down the walls before they painted them because the old scotch tape kept coming through.

Cathy McCoy-Morgan: I followed every single move they made. I bought all the Beatles books and magazines you could imagine. I knew their birthdays and their favorite colors, all that stuff. And I still do.

Cathy McCoy-Morgan engrossed in a Beatles fan magazine at Atlantic City, 1964.

Barbara Boggiano: At that time, that was our whole life—what they were doing, where they were going, when they were gonna be in concert—just following them along.

Wendi Tisland: I bought the fan magazines, listened to the music, talked about the Beatles, tried to dress like their girlfriends—not only did I love the Beatles, the girlfriends were fascinating, 'cause we were so envious of them. We wanted to be just like them, even though we were far from it!

Carol Cox: I started buying every single Beatle magazine, anything that had a mention of them. I had their pictures plastered all over my room, I listened to them all the time, I wore my Beatles T-shirt all the time. . . . I was twelve years old, I wanted to marry Paul—my whole life just changed. It revolved around the Beatles, period.

Carol Cox *in her bedroom with the Beatles enshrined on her walls.*

Deborah McDermott: When I think about being between the ages of 12 and 15, I think about this "perfect storm" of events: I was immature for my age, I was a young female teenager, and I was boy crazy. I was the perfect candidate to be a Beatles fan. Where did the music fit in? Certainly the appreciation of the music came later, but I almost think it was visceral reaction to *them*, more than to the music. Which is not to say that the music doesn't sustain me to this day. It's still the most wonderful music. But when you're 13 years old—I was reading the magazines, I was into every little nuance of their life. I was a like this crazed child!

Penny Wagner: And that's when my mother started buying me the albums, which I still have. I have all the originals. In fact, "I Want to Hold Your Hand" and the Beatles' first album are worn out. You can't even play it anymore. I wore it to the ground. *The Beatles' Second Album* is worn out . . . and I have the jackets that are all yellow.

Betty Taucher: The boys got into it. So you saw boys starting to play music—boys that were never into music were playing guitars and wanted to dance, and all of a sudden the boys were showing up at dances.

Charles Pfeiffer: Then I started playing guitar because of them. Realized that I loved music, and—just the whole British thing and their influence—out came the Stones, and The Who, and the Kinks. . . . I was infatuated with all of them. But I always felt the Beatles were the leaders. I was even kind of jealous that the Dave Clark Five or the Stones would get any more press than them. I thought it was really unfair.

Charles Pfeiffer and his newfound obsession.

Carolyn Long Paulk: I started this Beatles fan club at my elementary school. I was in the 8th grade at the time. I was collecting all of these Beatle bubble gum cards, which I still have. Tons of them. And my friends Connie, Becky, and Joy—we were all so into it. We were listening to Beatles albums 24/7. And we had just started to baby-sit, and we were playing them over and over—*Meet the Beatles* and *The Beatles' Second Album.* We wore them out. Plus we had a lot of 45s too.

Pete Kennedy: I've got my original little album that I kept my 45s in. I bought every one of their singles as they came out, 'cause it was just kind of a given that you would do that. And every time they were on *Sullivan,* of course you would watch that. And they were on *Shindig* one time, and of course you'd watch that. Your life kind of revolved around these appearances of new Beatle music. You would seek them out.

Penny Wagner: We dressed like them—I had a clique in Catholic grade school, and we got in so much trouble. We were called the Big Four; three other girls and me dressed like the Beatles. We got the hats, just like the hats they wore when they first came over from England—the girl with a lot of money got the hats for us. I wish to God I would have kept it. Buying the bubble gum, putting up that five-foot wall picture in my room, that rotten gum we had to chew for those pictures in the package. . . .

Barbara Boggiano: And *16* magazine at the time was *the* magazine. So as soon as I got my allowance, I was buying the latest edition. There was an article in *16* magazine, and it said would you like a Liverpool pen pal. They had hooked me up with a girl named Elizabeth from Liverpool, and a lot of my friends had gotten pen pals. That was exciting because I could actually write to someone who had been in the Cavern. All I could do was look at pictures, but she could write to me and tell me about just being down there, and experiencing that. And that to me was just fabulous.

* * *

On March 2, 1964, just over a week after returning to England from their triumphant visit to the U.S., the Beatles began filming their first scenes for their as-yet-untitled musical comedy feature. Of course, it would soon be titled *A Hard Day's Night*, inspired by one of Ringo's off-the-cuff remarks. It was written by fellow Liverpudlian Alun Owen, whose work the group enjoyed, and was directed by American Richard Lester.

Lester recreated much of the Beatles' world as it was during that slice of time in their lives—the close escapes from screaming mobs, the barrage of questions from reporters, and the visits to discotheques to let off steam. Lester also peppered the film with genuinely comic moments, vignettes, clever photography and editing techniques—-and, of course, lots of Beatles music.

The American fans would have to wait almost six months before the Beatles would return for their first full-length tour, but the group made news almost weekly, albeit the individual news items following their activities would vary in true significance. What was significant, though, was the steady rise of anticipation from mid-February through mid-August, for their return to the States. In the meantime, there was plenty going on.

* * *

Maggie Welch: In March, there was a closed-circuit presentation of the Washington Coliseum concert at two downtown theatres—the Denver and the Paramount. I think I still have my ticket from the Denver Theatre. It was as if everyone in the room was right there in the Coliseum. You could barely hear the Beatles because everybody was just screaming.

JoAnne McCormack: I went to St. Agnes in College Point. At that time it was an all-girl school. I hung out with a bunch of people there who were Beatles fans, too. I was the one known as the biggest Beatles fan. Being in Catholic school, we had to wear uniforms, and my wallet was thick with all Beatle pictures. And the Pope was coming into New York, and being Catholic school people, we had to go see him. I was 14 years old, and I'm sorry, but I didn't want to go see the Pope. There were four of us girls together, and one of my girlfriends had polio so she had a brace on her leg. So we're on the bus heading to St. Agnes and we're talking, and I was saying, "I'd rather see the Beatles than the Pope. Who wants to see the Pope? The Beatles are much better." To me, that's what you'd expect a normal 14- or 15-year-old girl to say. So we then get onto the train in the station, and we see this older lady who had been on the bus, we could tell she was listening to us. We're on one train, she's in another train, so she crosses to our train and sits right by us. Well the next day I get called down to the principal's office. This principal was new to the school, was a nun, and she was a real toughie. And I see my one girlfriend who was very introverted and I felt kind of protective towards her, and I see her sitting in the chair crying, so right away I'm getting annoyed.

So there I am with my blazer pocket ripped, I have a safety pin holding in my big wallet. She takes the wallet out of my pocket—you wouldn't get away with this stuff today, even in Catholic school. She takes it and goes through it, and there are all these Beatle pictures all over. She says, "Your mind's not in the right place! Is it true you'd rather see the Beatles than the Pope?" And my father always told me not to lie, plus I wouldn't because that would be disloyal to them! I looked her right in the eye and said, "Yes, Sister, I would." "That's it, you're suspended from class! I'm going to your parents. . . . " blah, blah. And I'm like, "What did I do?" I had to stay in the library the next day. A couple of the other teachers were in and out of the library and I could see them looking at me, like, "What are they doing to this kid?"

My mother came the next day, and she really listened to the authority figures, and said, "You know, she's not a juvenile delinquent" and this and that. And my other girlfriend had gotten called up too.

Her mother was British and she didn't take any nonsense, and she told the principal, "I'm a convert to the Catholic religion, I was brought up Anglican. I have respect for that habit you're wearing, but I have no respect for you as a woman, what you're doing to these kids is terrible." And my parents told me, "Don't worry, you're not in trouble with us. You didn't do anything wrong." I was always a big mouth about it, and if I got in trouble, I got in trouble.

* * *

On April 4th, while shooting *A Hard Day's Night*, the Beatles learned that they now occupied the top five spots on Billboard's Hot 100 chart:

1. Can't Buy Me Love
2. Twist and Shout
3. She Loves You
4. I Want to Hold Your Hand
5. Please Please Me

It was a feat that has not been equaled since. In addition, they had seven other songs listed in the Top 100 that same week.

The following week, on April 10th, Capitol released *The Beatles' Second Album*, only three months after releasing *Meet the Beatles*.

CHAPTER THREE

A Hard Day's Night

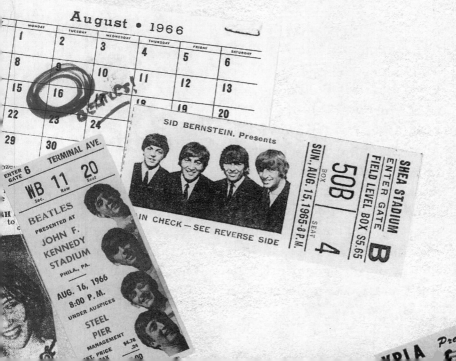

A s much as Beatles records were flying off the shelves in the spring of 1964, the wait for yet another big event was about to culminate with a new round of screaming fits by their ever-growing population of fans. On June 26th, United Artists released the U.S. soundtrack album for *A Hard Day's Night*.

The big event, however, was the July 6th premiere in London of the film itself. General release in the U.K. was scheduled for August 2nd. The American premiere took place on August 11th, with general release in 500 U.S. theatres the next day.

* * *

Mary Ann Collins: My understanding was that *A Hard Day's Night* was going to play at the Palace Theatre in Newport News. We had heard that was the first place on the East Coast that the Beatles' movie was going to play. I have no idea if that's really true or not, but that's what we had heard. But it was definitely the first place it was going to play in all of Tidewater. We had to go from Norfolk to the peninsula, which was about a 40-minute drive. I was working as a telephone operator at the time. I went to school and worked part time as a long-distance telephone operator. So I had a fair amount of money compared to some of my friends. I also had access to a car, my family was very generous, I didn't have my own car, but I had access to a car, and I was pretty much the

Tag given out with ticket purchase to see A Hard Day's Night.

one who always drove everywhere. So I was frequently the one who was orchestrating things or the one that was enabling things to take place.

We heard that the Beatle movie was going to come to the Palace Theatre, and we wanted to be there—myself and two other of my friends who were also Beatle nuts at the time. The three of us went over there with a portable radio, blanket, snacks, and we camped out overnight at the movie theatre to be the first ones to buy tickets to see the movie. This was just to *buy* tickets to see the movie. The movie wasn't going to actually play for two more weeks.

There was such a big deal made—they talked to us on the radio and everything—that two weeks later when the movie was going to actually play, we were so afraid that other people would have the same idea to get there really early. So this time we decided we would go over—I was working that night, I believe I got off at 10:00. I picked up the girls, we went over to the Palace Theatre, and we got there about 11:00 on the night before the movie was going to play the next morning. The first show was going to be around nine o'clock. And we each bought four tickets the two weeks before, because there were going to be four showings of the movie. So once again, we were the first ones in line to get into the movie and see the movie. They cleared out the theatre each time the movie was over, so we had to get back in line again and show our tickets.

And oh my lord, that movie—we thought we had died and gone to heaven! And to this day, I still think *A Hard Day's Night* is one of the coolest movies ever made. It was a great movie. I like *Help!* also, but *A Hard Day's Night* is the best. There was screaming, especially in the beginning, when you see them running toward the camera down the street—especially then, there was tons of screaming. But then as it went along it calmed down, because you wanted to hear them talk, hear their voices. So after the initial rush and excitement of seeing them on the screen, people did calm down.

JoAnne McCormack: August 14, 1964! We went to the Bel-Air Theatre in Valley Stream, New York, which is no longer there, and waited on line a while. We were seeing the second showing, and we went around to the back door of the theatre, and we could hear some of the talking in the film. We were saying, "Oh my God, that sounds like John!" "That sounds like Paul!" And we got in there, in the first row. And we sat and watched the screen and carried on as usual. At the end my girlfriend and I went up to the screen where they were flashing pictures of The Boys on the screen—we were up there kissing the screen. I remember going home and talking so fast and excited, and my mother was getting a little bent out of shape that I was so emotional and hyper. I talked to my girlfriend the next day and asked, "What did your mother say?" She said, "She laughed at me, gave me an aspirin, and sent me to bed!"

After we had seen it umpteen times, I'd go with three or four of my friends and we'd sit there and start doing the dialogue out loud. The funny thing is, nobody asked us to shut up!

Valerie Volponi: My friends and I went to see *A Hard Day's Night* 13 times. I took my shorthand book with me to the movie, and I took down the whole movie in shorthand—the dialogue. I really did this! And then

I came home and typed it up into a script. I actually used carbon paper to do this.

And then my friends and I would act out the movie in our backyard. We got quite good at it—we had the whole thing memorized. It was a lot of fun. It's very embarrassing now, but we had wonderfully creative minds back then. We had nothing to bore us, that's for sure.

Barbara Allen: In August, the film *A Hard Day's Night* was released, and that was a major thing. If you could have been there for that, you wouldn't have believed your eyes. That was another go-around because in Trenton, which was the closest city to where we were living—my mother had a classmate from way back in high school who owned the Greenwood Movie Theatre, which was right on the corner of Greenwood Ave. in Hamilton. And that's where the film ended up in that area. We were driven over to my grandparents who lived in the neighborhood, and went charging up to this small theatre. In those days everything was different, and this was just a little movie theatre on the corner—it wasn't the 309 Cinema with 50 different rooms. And it was a scene! There were these girls lined up in big lines screaming, clutching photos of their favorite Beatles, and all the trinkets, jumping up and down, and they had so many people trying to get into this, they had to stagger the showings. They couldn't have just one evening's showing, they had to go around the clock! The demand was unbelievable, and people were just going right back in and watching it six or seven times.

And when we got in there, the electricity in the air—people were screaming before the film even came on the screen! And the owner of this place, this poor man who would have been a middle-aged guy who never in his life—in fact my mother tells me that after this whole thing calmed down, he sold the cinema. He was undone by it! Anybody who was involved with 3,000 screaming girls—it really was something. And the movie came on, and it was pandemonium. I don't know how many shows I watched. We'd go over to my grandparents for a while, then come back, then go back again.

Carol Cox: There's a resort in California called Clear Lake, and the tickets for *A Hard Day's Night* were supposed to go on sale when we were on vacation. And I was really upset. Well, my dad was staying behind, so I came home from vacation and my dad surprised me. He had bought me—and I don't know where he got them from—two tickets to the local *A Hard Day's Night* premiere. I was beside myself. So I showed up at the premiere with all my Beatle gear and my buttons, bag of goodies, and everything else. It was one of the old-fashioned art deco theatres, with an actual stage, and they'd draw the curtains for the features. They had a whole build-up before the movie. They'd have people imitate the Beatles, and you'd win this little book called *Love Letters to the Beatles.* So me and three other girls around me imitated the Beatles onstage because I wanted the book so bad. And then when the movie came on they drew the curtains open and everybody started to scream. And you couldn't hear the dialogue 'cause we were all screaming. And when we weren't screaming, we were clapping. It was like being at a concert. Everybody was thrilled to see them. It was phenomenal. I can still remember that. And at the end, the whole feeling of elation as we all just watched them sing. It was so cool. To this day, *A Hard Day's Night* is my favorite movie. I watch it and I turn 12.

Betty Taucher: By the time the June came, there wasn't anybody in school who wasn't into that. I remember the movie cost a whole dollar, which was a lot when you think they cost 35 cents in that time frame. And I still have the ticket, 'cause it's the big yellow ticket with the Beatles on one end. And we all wore sweatshirts, even though it was in August, 'cause there weren't any t-shirts then, not like now,

Original theatre ticket to see *A Hard Day's Night* in Aynor, South Carolina.

that you can get with anybody and his uncle on them. The only thing that was around was the sweatshirts. And so we wanted to show our love for the Beatles, so we wore sweatshirts—in August. And our moms made us wear skirts 'cause we were going to the movies.

We screamed through the whole movie. My girlfriend fainted and we had to find her through all the people. Her radio fell, and the back came off, so we were crawling through all these people trying to find the pieces. We just dropped her in the seat, and dropped the radio in her seat, and as we found pieces we'd just drop them on it.

That's the only movie I can think of—it didn't happen with *Help!*—there was some of it, with certain close-ups—but during *A Hard Day's Night,* you screamed through the whole thing.

Charles Pfeiffer: When *A Hard Day's Night* came out we all stood in line like kids did everywhere and then we screamed all the way through the movie, like idiots. It didn't matter if you were a boy or a girl, you screamed for them.

Penny Wagner: My uncle ran a movie theatre in Kenosha. We must have seen *A Hard Day's Night*—I'm not exaggerating—about a hundred times, if not more, and *Help!* about 60 times. He let us keep going back to watch it. Every weekend my mother would ship us off, because we wanted to go see it again. The music is what we went for. All we'd do is scream. Just mention the name John, Paul, George, or Ringo, and we were screaming.

Maggie Welch: The minute "United Artists" came up on the screen, the screaming started, and it didn't stop until the movie was over.

The youth tickets were 60 cents, so it wasn't hard to scrape up the money. Some days we'd sit through it two or three times. And I saw that movie 26 times when it first came out, and I'm still not tired of it.

Ilona Gabriel: Every weekend, no matter how many times we saw it, we'd go to see *A Hard Day's Night.* We saw it well over a hundred times. One day several Beatle people were at the movie when there was a mechanical difficulty, and no sound. All of us provided the soundtrack, including sound effects. When someone shouted, "Where's the sound?" we responded,

"We're givin' it to ya!" A lot of the things we'd say to each other were quotes taken from *A Hard Day's Night* and *Help!*

A lot of the things we did on our time off were actually taken from the movies. We would take the subway to the Staten Island Ferry and go on the ferry and build a human pyramid out on the deck, figuring that's some crazy little stunt that the Beatles would do.

Linda Binns Liles: When *A Hard Day's Night* came out, we were in Cleveland, and I had gotten my uncle to agree to take me to it. And I paced the whole day waiting for him to get home. I was saying, "Come on! We've gotta go!" The poor man was going to choke while he was eating.

We got down there, and it was like a concert—the whole audience screamed the whole time during the movie. And I was thinking, I *met* them! I *talked* to them. And they're really nice guys!

Carolyn Long Paulk: On *A Hard Day's Night,* those girls were wearing a red tie and black & white herringbone jumper. My mom made me one of those, and I had a white Oxford cloth shirt, and my dad gave me this red tie he had. And whenever I wore that to school, I always had to wake him up early to tie my tie, 'cause I wanted to look like one of those girls with the long bangs and long hair. And mine was shoulder-length like that, and we thought we were so Jean Shrimpton/Liverpool. But it was a mod look from London.

Barbara Boggiano: I remember going to see *A Hard Day's Night* two or three times at the drive-in. My father agreed to take us, but it had to be the drive-in! You had to sit there with that crackling speaker, and you couldn't really listen to the music. And that's probably why we bugged my father to go three times.

CHAPTER FOUR

The 1964 Tour

As soon as details of the Beatles' first American tour were announced, fans scrambled to get their clutches on actual concert tickets. The tour was to begin on August 19th in San Francisco, making the interim between early spring and late summer feel like an eternity.

* * *

Maggie Welch: In March we heard about their big American tour, and that they were going to come to Colorado. Oh, my goodness. The tickets went on sale in March. I remember going downtown with my friends on the bus and standing in the snow to buy our tickets. Of course, it didn't matter because it was going to be at Red Rocks, which is a natural amphitheater, and it was general seating, first come, first served. But we wanted to get our tickets right away. So we stood there in the snow, had a wonderful time. We sang, giggled, told stories, basically acted like 13- and 14-year-old girls.

Then, of course, the long wait came, being broken only by the excitement of *A Hard Day's Night* being released.

Cathy McCoy-Morgan: I watched them on *Ed Sullivan*, absolutely. And I could not wait until they toured, until we could actually maybe get the chance to see them. I remember my cousin Judy had driven us down—she had this big white Chevy Impala convertible—and we drove down to Philadelphia. And she waited for us while we went in to get our tickets.

Barbara Allen: We ended up finding out about a ticket outlet in Trenton, where my father had his

Jumpin' Jellybeans—What a Sellout!

Beatle Fans Mob Convention Hall

By NELS NELSON

Somebody tried to knock down Convention Hall, but the cops wouldn't let them.

It happened yesterday afternoon, a little more than an hour after the box office opened to sell tickets to the Beatles' Sept. 2 concert.

The 12,000 available ducats had been whooshed up for the fastest sellout in Philadelphia show biz annals.

The doors were forced shut.

AND THERE ROSE from the environs of 34th St. and Convention Ave. the most horrendous chorus of caterwauling since Clyde Beatty got mad at his butcher and put his tigers on watercress salad.

Some 3,500 teenaged females yowled in scorned fury.

A dozen or more collapsed on the Convention Hall steps in tears. Others battered at the doors like the Belles of St. Trinian's. A pincers movement attacked the trade entrance on the side.

A few brave ones rat-a-tatted their fists on the cops' chests.

A LITTLE BLONDE in green Jamaica shorts ran up to the wall and crayoned naughty words directed at the ticket sellers.

"I'm gonna get a ticket but I don't know how," wailed a girl in a parochial school uniform.

"I'll just die if I don't get one," moaned a miss of about 15, sinking to the steps like a wounded turtledove.

ABOUT an hour after the ticket cupboard was revealed to be bare, a new wave of the spurned sisterhood mounted for an assault. It happened when an unsuspecting deliveryman approached the hall with a big pasteboard carton on his shoulder.

Disregarding the large letters on the carton that spelled "Scottissue," somebody yelled: "There's tickets in that box!"

The deliveryman was immediately engulfed in a stormy sea of upturned faces and clutching paws. A dozen policemen dashed to his rescue and escorted him inside.

It was a field day for girl-watchers. A stag line of nearly a hundred youths lingered around the perimeter, enjoying the spectacle.

THOUGH the ticket sale had been widely advertised to begin at 4:30 p.m., a small

CONTINUED ON PAGE 44

No Hawaii Hula-baloo

HONOLULU (UPI). — Beatles John Lennon and George Harrison, accompanied by two women, left Hawaii for Tahiti after a brief visit here. Only four squealing teenage girls watched them go.

THE LUCKY ONES?—These Lansdale girls, Arlene Godshall (left), and Cathy McCoy, didn't make trip in vain, as their pose of triumph, tickets aloft, indicates.

Cathy McCoy-Morgan (right) proudly displays her ticket to see the Beatles' Philadelphia concert in 1964.

business, and we walked over the bridge and went over there and got those tickets. That probably would have been in July, and this concert was in September. Then we brought the tickets home and everybody was very careful to protect them. They were under lock and key. It was like you had the Hope diamond. All the hysteria in the house was now "What if the house catches fire, and burns the Beatle tickets?" We were out of our minds and the parents were just beside themselves listening to this craziness. They couldn't believe it.

And then, it was early summer, when we weren't in school, we started to work on the little Beatles novel that we wrote. We illustrated it because two of the girls had art classes and we made up this story, and the funny thing was we took it up to New York the following year and took it to Murray the K's WINS office. We thought we'd have him give it to the Beatles, can you imagine? We took the train and my mother took us up there and we dropped it off, and we kept copies. When they released *Help!* there was a funny similarity, and I'm sure it had no connection, but we wanted to think it did. It got into kind of a fantasy where they had read the story and had taken it from there. So those were funny things we used to think about.

* * *

On July 20th, a month before the American tour was to begin, Capitol released yet another hatchet job of an album, *Something New*. It actually consisted mostly of the songs Capitol had removed from the B-side of the British LP of *A Hard Day's Night*, which it replaced with several instrumental tracks from the film's background score. This made *Something New* anything but.

The first U.S. tour schedule consisted of 25 concerts to be played in 31 days. It had the Beatles criss-crossing North America in a rather haphazard fashion, basically working from west to east, back to the mid-west, then to the north into Canada, back down south to Florida, and so on, in a dizzying zig-zag of travel routes.

It all began when they arrived in San Francisco on August 19th, with only hours to spare before their first concert of the tour at the Cow Palace.

* * *

Paula Myers: We found out where they were staying, at the Fairmont Hotel. We went there, my sister and I, and our dad took us there. He had sculptured a bust of Paul, and so we took it there to the hotel and gave it to probably the concierge, and told him to give it to Paul, which he probably didn't, ya know. I don't think they'd want to be lugging around all this stuff that the fans wanted to give them every place they went. But it was a really nice sculpture.

Lila Kraai: We got into a press conference at the Cow Palace in '64. Two friends wanted to go, and they lived on the other side of town. They made all of the arrangements. Basically, one of the girls' fathers had some kind of connections, and he's the one that got us in. All we had to do was give the key to the Beatles from the city of Los Gatos. We had another friend make a key, and we painted it gold and put a red ribbon on it. And we had the mayor and town council sign it. I would say the majority of people there were from the press. I didn't know what I was getting into. I just sort of went where they told me to go, and stood there and couldn't really believe what was happening.

I was in awe. The third girl I was with had the key, and I'm the one who had to nudge her and say, "Give them the key! Give them the key!" because she was totally in awe too. She held the key—it was a big thing—and she was holding it and holding it, looking at Paul and drooling, and I had to nudge her.

Lila Kraai's photo of the Beatles' San Francisco press conference, just after she and friends presented them with the key to the city of Los Gatos.

We saw the whole press conference. I could never understand how George's body was held up on those skinny legs! I feel real lucky that I was able to see them at the beginning of their stardom. By '66, I just don't think they were into meeting the fans anymore.

Dale Ford: The radio was the way you got your tickets. They'd advertise and told you what you had to do. You had to send a self-addressed stamped envelope to a certain place, and they told you when they'd announce the address and where to send the money. I was totally tuned in with my paper and pen in hand, and I got the thing off that day. It was like $6.50 or something like that, and I got two. We ended up on the main floor, about halfway back. I went with my boyfriend at the time, another friend and his girlfriend. I was just so excited and I could hardly stand it, and I had never been to a concert in my life. This was my first experience. I didn't know what to expect, except I knew everybody there had flash cameras. A lot of them were using the flashbulbs that pop in and you had to use a new flashbulb for each picture. I think we had an Instamatic, and we took pictures, and I still have them. You couldn't see much because we were halfway back and of course the light only lights up the people in front of you.

When they finally came out, it was deafening, just absolutely deafening! Nothing but shrill screams, I didn't even know what song they were playing until maybe 30 seconds before the song ended, then I finally caught wind of what they were singing. But nobody seemed to care! They just wanted to see the Beatles. And this whole place was totally illuminated with everybody's flashes going off. And all this screaming. I was going nuts. I was screaming my head off like a banshee. I couldn't see because we were on the main floor, not in any kind of elevated section, so I told my boyfriend—who actually turned out to be my husband later—since everybody was already standing on their chairs, I said, "You stand on the chair and I'm gonna get up on your shoulders." And there was no crowd control because these poor ushers, they didn't know what hit them. They didn't have enough, they didn't have any discipline whatsoever.

Lila Kraai: I had promised myself I was not going to scream. It was just like I got caught up in this wave of screams. And all the chairs were wooden chairs, and we were standing on them. I don't think I'd do that today! You could tell what songs they were singing, but you couldn't follow the music very well. I guess the thing that strikes me the most is how together they were. They fed off of each other's comments.

Paula Myers: We weren't very close to the stage, so that was kind of aggravating. There was always too much screaming. We didn't scream, we weren't that kind of fans. We actually wanted to hear the music. So we were really aggravated by all the people screaming.

Dale Ford at the Beatles' 1964 Cow Palace concert.

Dale Ford: The crowd just did what they wanted to do, so I got up on my boyfriend's shoulders for 30-second glimpses and to take pictures throughout the concert. And it really didn't last very long! But you just knew you were in the presence of greatness. Even back then, when groups would come and go, one-time hit wonders. But I just knew it. I was thinking to myself, "Dale, savor this moment. This is gonna go down in history." And it did!

* * *

The Beatles moved on from San Francisco to Las Vegas for a concert at Convention Hall on August 20th. On the 21st, they were off to the Coliseum in Seattle. Claudia Kilburn confronted a big phobia in order to witness the Beatles' helicopter flying into town.

* * *

Claudia Kilburn: It was the first and last time I've ever been to the Space Needle. I was always afraid of heights. I was so excited to get a glimpse of them, I took that chance and kind of held back—I wasn't hanging over the edge. But we did see their helicopter land on the Edgewater Hotel. Their rooms overlooked the water on Elliot Bay, and they fished with fishing poles out their hotel room. I didn't see that, but that was on the news.

The concert was the very same day. I remember how crazy everybody was, screaming at all the music. To me, all the noise was a big disruption. If everyone was quiet, we could have enjoyed the concert that much more. But everybody was screaming and crying. I was emotional, I was excited, but I didn't scream. I don't recall crying. My older cousin went with me, and she was four years older and not a real big Beatles fan, so that might have kept me in check. I didn't want her to think I was some kind of idiot carrying on! It was something that I'll always remember.

* * *

On August 22nd, the Beatles crossed over the border into Vancouver, Canada for a concert at Empire Stadium. The following day, they were in Los Angeles, performing at the famed Hollywood Bowl.

August 26th brought them to one of their more unique venues, the Red Rocks outdoor amphitheater outside of Denver. Maggie Welch had waited five long months between the day she bought her ticket and the day of the concert.

* * *

Maggie Welch: Then the big day came. I think the poor fathers drew lots [to drive us]. Some people kept out at Red Rocks all night. We had to climb a huge flight of stairs to get to the theatre. At noon this guy with a big megaphone came and said, "All right, now we're going to walk, I repeat walk, down to the theatre." And being good little girls, we started to walk until we thought to ourselves, "What are we doing? This is general admission!" And everybody broke into a dead run like they were doing the marathon, and hit those stairs. And here's this poor ticket taker besieged by girls, and I thought, I'm not just going to stand here. So I ran into the theatre and sat on John's side, because he was my favorite. A few minutes later my friends came—they knew I'd break my neck to get a good seat.

The concert wasn't going to start until 8:00 so we had a lot of time to kill. So there was a lot of talking around, getting to know people, buying the programs, ooh-ing and ahh-ing over the photographs. When they brought Ringo's drum out and turned it around to where it said "The Beatles," that was good for at least 20 minutes of screaming.

Finally, after sitting through all these warm-up acts, at ten o'clock in the evening, the announcer said "And now . . . " You could hear a pin drop. And then he said. "The Beatles!" and the place just erupted. I went to watch John Lennon sing "Twist and Shout" live. There isn't anybody in the world who's ever going to sing that song better than he did.

There's a little town, about five or seven miles away from Red Rocks, called Morrison, and legend says that they could hear the screaming very clearly.

Being lucky enough to be in the first row, I got to hear them really being themselves. And I had been pre-warned about that, because I stole my brother's *Playboy* magazine with their interview in it. I knew they weren't these really clean-cut, goody-goody boys that Brian Epstein was promoting them to be. So I wasn't surprised by their off-color remarks they made to each other, and the fun that they were poking at each other. I'm so glad that I saw them at that period because by 1966, they weren't having any fun at all.

Red Rocks just has a little railing that goes around the front of the stage. And they had a few policemen stationed by the railing, but they sat down so we wouldn't have to try to peek over their heads. Actually, everyone was very good, there was the obligatory throwing of the jelly beans. I had binoculars, and when I had those on, and looked at them, it was like it was almost too personal. I could see every single pore in their faces, practically. I wasn't a screamer, I only screamed when they started singing "Things We Said Today," because it was one of my favorite songs and I never thought they'd do it in concert. And I screamed more out of surprise than anything else. I didn't come there to jump up and down and forget, I came there to watch and see, and be a witness to this extraordinary event that I might never have a chance to have again, and sure enough I never did.

And having been there, and especially being that close, the energy that these people exuded from the stage was not to be believed. And their charisma, how relaxed they were with each other, and with their abilities, it was really something to see. They had a very particular energy they shared between themselves, and I was so close to them that I could feel that happening in my body.

And it was an extraordinary experience. Their presence and charm was so immense that they just couldn't contain it in one little space.

George at one point said, "Anyone know what the next song is?" Paul took a little look at his Hofner and told him what the next song was going to be. Paul slipped on a jelly bean and he really nearly did go down. He had to put his hand on the floor to prevent himself from falling flat on his "arse." He got back up, jumped back into the song, and John practically fell over—it was the funniest thing he'd ever seen in his life. He was pointing his finger and laughing. He started playing again but they knew nobody could hear them. It was almost as if with all the confidence that was on the stage, George would rather have been anywhere else in the world than where he was. A little bit awkward, maybe a tad out of place, and not real confident about himself. I think that was very clear. Lennon-McCartney is a pretty tough act to follow.

They absolutely loved it and wanted to come back. It's a really beautiful place to see anybody. But that wasn't their decision, and they never came back. But I'm so grateful to have seen them. I was on a huge high for quite some time. It was an extremely energizing and enlightening performance.

That's when I really started buying tons and tons of books, and before that I started subscribing to *Beatles Monthly*, which was such a better magazine than anything we had in the States. I took a double subscription out, because I said, when I'm a grandma, and I'm feeling a little blue—sometimes the past is the greatest vacation spot in the world—I can just drag these out and take a look through them, and I can be 13 again. I wasn't thinking as a collector, it's just because I thought it would be nice to have a clean copy when I was old. So that gave me another copy that I could just completely cut up and destroy, plaster all over my locker and my room.

* * *

The Beatles continued traveling eastward, playing The Gardens in Cincinnati on August 27th. Then it was back to New York City, for two concerts at Forest Hills tennis stadium in Queens.

The group's New York visit this time had them staying at Manhattan's Delmonico Hotel on Park Avenue and 59th Street. Their arrival created yet another scene of mayhem on the streets of New York. Wooden police barricades, so useful for crowd control outside the Plaza back in February, this time kept thousands of fans from blocking Park Avenue traffic entirely.

It was during this brief stay at the Delmonico that New York radio's awesome influence with teenagers created some truly magical moments. WABC set up a temporary remote studio in the hotel, with DJs Scott Muni, Cousin Brucie, and news director Jim Gordon reporting live on the excitement generated by the Beatles' presence. The DJs reported on the size and delirium of the crowd below, but also communicated directly to them—not via loudspeakers or megaphones, but right on the air. Untold numbers of the girls on the street below had their transistor radios on and set to WABC, enabling the on-air personalities to engage in a true dialogue with them. Muni served as cheerleader while Brucie offered up-to-the-minute details of the Beatles' activities, and Ingram played several of the station's jingles for the crowd sing-alongs. The sound of thousands of young listeners gleefully singing, cheering, and screaming in reaction to various cues and Beatles-related announcements from the DJs, was nothing short of breathtaking.

WABC also aired the big pre-concert story that day. A zealous fan had ripped Ringo's St. Christopher's medal from around his neck the night before, prompting the radio station to implore its return. About 150 fans showed up with medals of that ilk, but sixteen-year-old Angie McGowan of Manhattan rightly claimed to have the real thing. She returned it to Ringo on the air, as Cousin Brucie guided the two through the somewhat awkward meeting. It ended with a kiss on the cheek for the benefit of the press photographers.

Later that day, the group took a helicopter ride over Forest Hills stadium and the World's Fair, and would return by helicopter to the stadium for their concert the next day.

* * *

Valerie Volponi: Four of us bought our tickets and counted the days until August 28th at Forest Hills. We actually went to the stadium early in the day, and we walked around the neighborhood and found a place to have lunch. We all had our best outfits on . . . hopefully we would be seen by the Beatles, maybe. We still have our outfits packed away. And they came in by helicopter, which was very exciting and caused a lot of screaming. I can still see the helicopter circling outside the stadium.

I have my diaries here. It's very interesting to go back and read these. I have this diary from 1964 and I have these Beatles baseball cards glued in here, all over this diary:

> The concert was just fab. I can't believe it was really them. For once we saw them live, not on any screen or in a picture. They moved around much more than on TV. Ringo can really play the drums! . . . They wore sort of purple silver suits with velvet collars. . . . My sister Pam went hysterical, and we had to calm her down. I couldn't laugh, cry, or scream. I just stared. . . .

Kathy Albinder: Everybody went out and we all bought new clothes. We had outfits we were wearing for the concert. And it was all English stuff, anything that was English. The long ties, and the jumpers, and the high socks that all the English girls were wearing—we were wearing them. Long hair—and my hair was curly, but I ironed it so it was straight. And I had never done that before but everybody wanted to have straight hair. So I had straight hair for a few hours before it got too humid out there. I wore a blue jumper, I still remember that.

Everybody was screaming so you could hardly hear anything. It was very loud. But again it was a lot of fun. I didn't do that kind of stuff, I didn't go to concerts like that. But concerts weren't really anything like that before.

JoAnne McCormack: I was way up in the nosebleed seats. About halfway or three quarters through the show I just suddenly felt myself going backwards. The next thing I know I was sitting in a lady's lap behind me. I had fainted. I think the emotions, the hot August night, it was the first time I saw them, it was exciting. Some girl jumped onstage, and started dragging George—I don't know where she was trying to take him—but she was dragging him towards Paul. Security got up there real quick and got rid of her.

Valerie Volponi: I remember seeing a lot of girls who ran through the barricades. And all the police had to hold them back. The newspaper the next day really exaggerated. I would say maybe 20 or 30 girls ran through, and the newspaper said many more, maybe 80 or 100.

* * *

The Beatles' next gig was in Atlantic City on August 30th, at Convention Hall.

* * *

Claire Krusch: In the summer of 1964, the Democratic National Convention was in Atlantic City. And our dad was working for New Jersey Bell at the time, and they sent him to Atlantic City for the whole summer, to do some of the technical phone work at Convention Hall, and said, you can bring your whole family with you. They put us up in a hotel, but we never got to see our dad cause he was working fifteen or twenty hours a day. And my mom and my older sister and myself went down at the end of July or beginning of August, so we were there for five weeks. Word got out that the Beatles were coming to Convention Hall, where the Miss America Pageant is, August 30th. We bought tickets sometime in the middle of August, and the tickets were five dollars apiece. I believe they're still somewhere in the attic of my house where I grew up. And every time I go to see my mom, I spend a little more time there looking, 'cause I'm determined to find them.

Suzanne Milstead: I had a nephew named Mark who was from California. He came to stay with us that summer, and was around my age. We got tickets and went to the concert in Atlantic City. Before the concert, we were standing waiting for the Beatles to come out of a department store. A crowd was gathering in front of this very large department store that had plate glass windows. The buzz went through the crowd that they were in the store, and the crowd kept building, and building. Then a limousine came, and somebody came out of the store, and I believe it was them. And the plate glass window broke. We were pushed against them so tightly that they broke. The crowd was just pushing and pushing. The limo was there and the doors were open, and I think the policemen took them somewhere else. And the doors of the limo were open, and people were just pushed right through the limousine and got out on the other side. I got my leg cut. Everyone was pushed down the side street, and there were first aid booths set up. Mark and I got separated. I went to the first aid booth where they patched my leg.

Claire Krusch: The convention was over about three days before the concert, so my parents let us stay with them—my sister, a friend of ours, and myself. I still remember to this day walking in Convention Hall, and seeing that drum set on the stage. Here I am all of 13, and it took my breath away. Seeing "Ludwig" on the side, and "The Beatles" across the bass drum, it just blew me away.

The act before the Beatles was the Righteous Brothers. Then there was an intermission. And during the time the Righteous Brothers were singing, rumors started going around that the Beatles were up in the balcony watching them. And of course nobody was paying attention to the Righteous Brothers onstage, everybody started looking up at the balcony. And whether it was true or not I have no idea.

There wasn't screaming yet, but there was so much energy, you could just feel it. You could feel the electricity in the air, the adrenaline rush. It was incredible. Then when whoever it was introduced the Beatles, the place went wild. You couldn't hear a thing. Every girl that was around us—and I don't remember any guys—everybody got up on their chairs, and we just screamed our heads off. I wrote down every song they played on the back of my ticket.

We wore yellow canary dresses so that the Beatles would see us, and would stand out. And apparently everyone else had the same idea. And of course you covered yourself with Beatle buttons. We were probably in row 64 or 65, not the worse seats, but not the best. If everyone had sat down, we would have gotten a clear view of them. But as soon as those guys came onstage, the place went nuts, and everybody stood on their seats and screamed—just like you see on all those clips. That's exactly the way it was. Acoustic wise, with the high ceiling, it was still deafening. This was the first concert that my parents let us go to unchaperoned, so they were wrecks. They were very worried about us. Girls were fainting, and they're bringing people out on stretchers out to the boardwalk and putting them in ambulances. And we later learned our parents were out there watching this whole thing unfold.

The Beatles never talked, I don't remember hearing them introduce themselves, no "it's so great to be in Atlantic City," I don't remember any of that. They basically sang for about 30 minutes. It was organized chaos, if that's possible.

Carol Moore: And the concert itself of course, you couldn't hear anything for the screaming. It was a huge hall, and we were pretty far from the stage. And at that point I thought the screaming was a bit much. I was somewhat more reserved at that point. It wasn't until the second concert, at the Paramount, that I started screaming!

Claire Krusch: I remember thinking, "I am breathing the same air that the Beatles are breathing!" I just thought that was so cool, the most wonderful thing in the world. I always say that was one of the coolest days of my life.

* * *

The Beatles next performed at Philadelphia's Convention Hall on September 2nd.

* * *

Barbara Allen: On the 2nd, which I think was a school day, [my friend's father] Mr. Hollanbach drove all of us down to Philadelphia. It would have been four of us, and my sister, so that's five girls in the car. He took us down to the old Convention Hall, and parked the car. I don't even know what he did with himself when we went inside, because at that point all of the tickets had been sold out. There were huge lines of girls. Some guys, but mostly young girls. We got inside, and our seats were towards the middle, and Sandy thought that wasn't good enough. So we followed her up to the press box, and she talked her way into the press box.

And we ended up close to the stage with the press. And Harry Harris, who wrote for the *Inquirer* and who interviewed us for the article, was sitting nearby. And that's how we hooked up with him, cause he was a foe!

Anybody who wrote negatively about the Beatles was considered horrible. And in those days there was a very strict dress code in our area, influenced by the Philadelphia Catholic schools, I think. The conservatives were the cool kids, and you had to wear certain colors. You had to wear cranberry and navy blue, and the boys wore desert boots, the girls wore penny loafers, so you had to wear these certain colors and you had to dress accordingly. And if you wore white socks, it was considered a terrible social dress faux pas. So anyone who wrote disparagingly of the Beatles was called a jive or a something or other and "he probably wears white socks."

And Harry Harris wrote a commentary after the Beatles were on TV and said that Mitzi Gaynor was better than the Beatles. And that inflamed everybody. Everything was at a fever pitch. Anything that wasn't them was no good, in our eyes. They got us going!

Somehow we got into conversation, and we couldn't believe that we were actually meeting our foe, and then I guess there was a lot of laughing, 'cause we couldn't believe we had met him, the irony of the whole thing.

What happened next was they started to announce that the Beatles were gonna be on the stage. And that is when the place went insane. We were standing on chairs, and we were hitting the men who were in the press box—these older gentlemen, and we were hitting them and screaming, pounding on them—it was unbelievable. You couldn't hear the music, it was deafening. According to Mr. Hollanbach, who was outside, it was a "deafening roar."

We were in front of Paul. You were almost like in a state of shock, because of the build up of all these

Philadelphia Inquirer *columnist Harry Harris describes encountering fan Barbara Donini (later Allen) and friends in the press box of the Philadelphia concert.*

months of wanting to see them, and waiting for this. And now here they were in front of you, and it was only going to be for a half hour. And I think there were girls trying to jump on the stage too, 'cause that would have been the ultimate, to jump on one of them. This was never an overtly sexual thing, it was more like you want to hug them and kiss them—there was a lot of that kind of wonderful affection that was in our heads.

Now that you're older and you're a lot more tuned into emotion and a state of mind, some people would say it was an out-of-body experience, almost—taken to a whole different place. And it's pure emotion that does that.

Cathy McCoy-Morgan: I went with my older sister Sharon. She remembers taking me into the rest room to put water on my face 'cause I was so hysterical, basically.

Barbara Allen: The girls who cried were not in our group. It was more screaming, and jumping up and down, pounding on the backs of the adults who were sharing the box with us. We were just so overwhelmed with our emotions. You were just so happy you were delirious. Then there were girls who did cry and get very emotional . . . the thing that the Beatles evoked was really something. How does it sound to men? From what I understand, the longer they performed and were subjected to all of this, the more reclusive they wanted to become. I don't think they expected the reaction of the fans that they got. I think they were sort of amazed. I think the promoters were amazed too.

* * *

After the Philadelphia concert, the Beatles headed to the Midwest and back into Canada, for seven concerts in as many days. On September 3rd, they played at the State Fair Coliseum in Indianapolis, then proceeded to Milwaukee for a concert the next day at the Auditorium.

* * *

Penny Wagner: My cousin, who was 16, surprised me with tickets. And my mother said I couldn't go. And I had a conniption for, like, four months. I cried and cried and cried. And she finally allowed me. My cousin said she would be responsible for me, and she was 16, about to be 17, and I was just 12 years old.

There were more girls than boys, by maybe a 4 to 1 ratio. And the boys were holding their ears. I remember seeing that a lot.

I remember ripping part of my hair out of my head, screaming, non-stop screaming—we couldn't talk after the concert we were screaming so bad.

After the concert—we wore dresses; skirts and white blouses, and saddle shoes, believe it or not. We chased the limousine. It was my cousin's idea. We climbed over a fence with our dresses on, chased the limousine, almost *caught* the limousine—it was going the wrong way down a street here in Milwaukee—we saw them wave at us. I'll never forget that as long as I live. There were girls coming from everywhere trying to get to that car. But the cops nailed us. The cops grabbed both of us, then called our parents. And I got a good licking when I got home!

* * *

The next several stops included Chicago and Detroit, then a side trip across the Canadian border:

September 5th Chicago—International Amphitheater
September 6th Detroit—Olympia Stadium
September 7th Toronto—Maple Leaf Gardens
September 8th Montreal—Forum

The dizzying nature of the Beatles' itinerary then brought them down to Jacksonville, Florida for a concert at the Gator Bowl on September 11th, immediately followed by a trip to Boston for a gig at the Boston Garden on the 12th.

Fourteen-year-old Janet Pickell (now Lessard) and her friend decided to use a bit of ingenuity to secure themselves tickets to the Boston concert.

* * *

Janet Lessard: When we found out they were coming to Boston, we were just beside ourselves at that point. We had never been to a concert, I can't even remember anything actually being called a concert at that point. The question was how were we going to get tickets? So my girlfriend and I decided we would write to the paper (the *Record American*, before it was taken over by the *Boston Herald*) and volunteer our services as newspaper reporters. We thought of it as kind of a joke. We thought, wouldn't it be funny if it caught somebody's eye, and sure enough, it did. We got a call from the editor, and he sent us press passes, and we got fourth row seats to the concert. We actually got passes to the press conference at the Madison Hotel in the afternoon. But my mother wouldn't let me go. That she kind of put her foot down on, she was a little nervous about that, but she did allow us to go to the concert at night.

The girl I was going to the concert with came to my house early in the morning. We had our hearts set on going to the Madison Hotel for the press conference, but again, being 13 and 14 years old, my mother wouldn't allow us to just get on a train and go into Boston, so we would have to rely on an adult bringing us. And there was no one who could bring us in the afternoon. My father did drive us to the concert though, and waited around the corner somewhere.

It was very exciting just going into this building, which I had never been to, and seeing so many young people in one place. And you compare it to today—there was no crowd control, no pushing and shoving, no fights breaking out, nothing going on that we wouldn't want to be going on.

We sat next to Arnie Ginsberg who at that point was one of the DJs in Boston who was playing Beatle records. It was a nice way to get a good seat, I must say! The kids in our class were all happy for us. So that was phenomenal. That I do remember. The other stuff is a little vague and hazy. But I do remember that concert.

* * *

Brian Tourville was only 12 at the time, but the significance of the event was not lost on him.

* * *

Brian Tourville: I was there early, Mom dropped me at the Garden. The first time ever to Boston.

I was the first one at the door, first into the Garden. I went to the stage to see the equipment—the drum set of Ringo's and "The Beatles" emblazoned on the front head.

I had a sixth row seat, courtesy of a real estate friend of my dad's friend who had season box seats at the Garden and knew the manager! When they took to the stage, as John came out he scanned the crowd and caught my sight. He said, "Hello!" John was such a magnificent presence.

Janet Lessard: When they announced the Beatles and they came on the stage, everybody stood up and pushed toward the stage. It was like a wave of people just pushing to the stage, so we were kind of wrapped up in the crowd and we found ourselves at the base of the stage, looking up at the four of them playing.

Brian Tourville: And the screaming! It began at the rear of the Garden and rolled forward toward the stage. I could *see it* coming! I got trapped by the crowd, just to John's right. The din hit the stage and the vocals disappeared instantly, leaving the Beatles "standing there," as would people on a subway waiting for the next stop. John immediately looked toward Paul and George, using body language to maintain the beat until the shrieking "cloud" subsided. This really annoyed him!

Janet Lessard: You could hear nothing [from them]. I defy anyone who says they were there and could hear them sing. They could have been whistling Dixie and you never would have known the difference because you could not hear them. But we could see them, and you hear the noise of the instruments, but you could not hear their voices. And it just went so fast. It was like watching *The Ed Sullivan Show.* They came out, they danced around like they used to do a little bit, cracked jokes, which you couldn't really hear, and joked among themselves basically, more than with us, and it certainly wasn't polished. They didn't have it down pat at that point.

For some reason, the reaction, after listening to the music you just break out into tears. You'd be so wrung out emotionally that you'd just start crying.

It was just a din for those 45 minutes. Screaming, crying, between that and the amplification they had on the stage, which was very primitive compared to today's standards, it was basically just being there and watching them, cause you didn't really hear anything. But that was fine with us. When it was over and they left, we went up on the stage.

I do remember afterwards a lot of the girls were crying and just kind of milling around. The cops were very nice to us, very patient with us, and finally got us out of the building.

It was completely unlike us. I can't understand why we were doing it. I asked my mother today, "Can you remember anything I said?" and she said, "All I can remember is when you came home, I asked you how it was and you burst into tears. And for one week I would say to you 'What was the concert like?' and you would start talking and just start crying." My brother and sister got quite a kick out of this too. And I know other girls who went through this with us say the same thing.

We went in the following Sunday morning to the paper, and one of the beat writers interviewed my friend and I. And he actually wrote the article. Those were not my words word for word. There were certain phrases that I recognized as mine. Some of the other things I think he took a little liberty with. I do remember reading it at that time and saying "Gee, I don't think I said that," and "I think Debbie said that," but he got the gist of it. We were actually very popular for about a month, when people found out about that, and they were very happy for us.

Boys liked them too. There wasn't any kind of jealousy. They actually enjoyed them. They immediately adopted the hairstyles and the clothes, and when they got a little older formed their own groups. So it was more of a universal thing. It wasn't like when Frank Sinatra came out, it was the young women, the bobby-soxers, went crazy over him. But it was basically the women. Elvis the same. It was basically the girls who would swoon over him. Whereas I think when the Beatles came out, at least in the beginning, the boys enjoyed them as much as the girls.

To me, it was the first album, the second album, the movie *A Hard Day's Night.* I think that was the thing that attracted the younger kids. There was a lot of innocence there when they first started. And even the parents weren't upset as you think they would be, of the kids copying this look and listening to this music. It wasn't threatening, and I think even the adults weren't threatened. When they were on the *Sullivan* show the second

Famous 4 Are 'Gear' To Teen Girl Reporter

By JANE PICKELL

I can't begin to tell you what it was like at Boston Garden Saturday night, except to say that when it was all over, I went down to the lobby and cried. I couldn't help it. I had seen them in person, and I couldn't believe it.

GEORGE HIT THRICE

They're just so FAB I thought I was dreaming. They're GEAR . . . a real Cassius Clay type of superlative. They're so clean, so enjoyable. They're having a ball and they want everyone else to be happy too.

George got hit three times . . . with a popcorn ball, an apple and some jelly BABIES. I think he's the nicest, but I'm prejudiced. I think he's the best looking and the most talented.

The kids enjoyed seeing them more than hearing them. When John was fooling around, clapping his hands, I thought I would die. And Paul got down on his knees, with John telling

(Janet Pickell is a 14-year-old freshman at Bishop Fenwick High School who lives at 70 County Way ext., Beverly. Her credentials consist of several hundred Beatles pictures, a lock of John Lennon's hair, and a pair of brown eyes, the same color as George Harrison, her favorite. She volunteered to cover the Beatles show as a teenage reporter.)

him how handsome he was. It was fabulous.

I think Paul is the cutest and the most popular. Everyone knows John is the smartest. George has the thickest

Janet Pickell, 14

Janet Lessard as a guest columnist describing the excitement of the '64 concert at the Boston Garden.

Beatles 'Fab' Says Admirer

Continued from Page 3

hair, and it's dreamy. I think Ringo is lonely, but he's so nice.

Paul told us, "Go ahead and scream—we love it." We could read their lips, so we knew what they were saying. If we didn't scream, they'd be in trouble. If you just sit there, they think you don't like them.

We like them because they're clean, and they're funny without being rude. They're not "pretty boys." They sing songs teenagers like. George says himself: "We're not the best musicians in the world, but we're passable."

Those psychologists trying to see what makes them tick are awful. Paul says half of them have no degrees. I almost died when George sang "Roll Over Beethoven." That was my favorite. I wanted to run up and touch him, but I didn't dare.

Afterwards, the police let us

time, my parents sat with me. Even my mother found them non-threatening and she kind of liked them, and my father—well, I wouldn't say he liked them, but he certainly didn't run out of the room.

* * *

After Boston, the Beatles headed South again for a gig at the Baltimore Civic Center on September 13th. Linda Cooper was determined to make up for an earlier lost opportunity.

* * *

Linda Cooper: Of course, I wanted to go down to the Washington Coliseum concert, and my mother said no way, 'cause it was in a horrible part of town, and she said "You're not gonna go down there to see that crap." So of course I was miserable. And then I heard they were coming back in September to the Baltimore Civic Center, and of course I begged and pleaded, and she said no way. And I had a bunch of friends at school who had gotten tickets, and I was just devastated. I wanted to go and they were going to be back again so soon.

It was on a Sunday, the day they were going to be there, and we didn't have tickets or anything, but Sharon and I ganged up on her father, and said, "We just want to breathe the air that they're breathing!"

So we got him to drive us to Baltimore. There were six of us. So we got in the station wagon and drove down to Baltimore. And we were driving around the Civic Center, and we knew the Beatles were at the Holiday Inn. We were just kind of walking around, we just wanted to be there.

So I walked into the Baltimore Civic Center, up to the box office, and laughingly said, "Do you have any tickets?" And we got tickets in the *front row*. Three dollars and seventy-five cents a ticket. We sat in the front row—we were in the paper the next morning. My mother couldn't believe it, 'cause I had to call her and tell her we weren't coming back right away! I was terrified because I thought she was going to be angry with me. She actually was really cool about it, and the next day we were in the *Baltimore Sun*. It was the three of us, we had the black turtlenecks and our skirts, and our boots, so we were doing our whole outfit thing. We sat next to a disc jockey who was traveling with them, and talked to him. And I had a ring that I wore, and I gave it to him, and he gave it to Paul . . . and when they came out and started "Twist and Shout," Paul had my ring on his pinkie. I was in seventh heaven! And there we were in the front row of the Baltimore Civic Center. And they only played 35 minutes. And we had to sit through Jackie De-Shannon and the Exciters, and everyone was just dying, I mean nobody cared that they were there.

The crowd was just hysterical. And I didn't pay attention to them because it was such a short period of time. But it was loud, there was lots of stuff being thrown—you'd get hit in the back with jelly beans, and lots of stuffed animals—but they just were so mesmerizing. And their voices were so good and clear! I didn't scream, I cried. I wanted to hear! It was crazy. I loved them, but I loved their music. I wanted to hear it!

That was my first experience. And the fun thing is, later, we got in the car and kind of drove around the Holiday Inn, and they were out and about on the balcony. And we were yelling from the car until the police came and made us go away.

Mary Ann Collins: I won my concert tickets through a contest. The same radio station that had come over to interview us, WGH—they had obtained 50 pairs of tickets, and they were gonna have a drawing from all the letters and postcards that came in. I went to a small Catholic high school. There was a core group of us—we were definitely the "Beatle nuts" or "Beatlemaniacs" of the school. Everybody knew that. My friends and I decided we'd get more bang for our buck if we sent postcards, 'cause we'd be able to send more postcards because they were cheaper. The radio station chose 48 letters and 2 postcards. Both of the postcards were ours! So we were actually entitled to 2 pairs of tickets. Well, unbelievably, no one else's parents allowed them to go. By now I was 17, a senior in high school, I had a job, I was responsible, my mother trusted me. Whether she was permissive, or knew I wanted to do this so badly, she allowed me to go.

But I had to find someone else to go with me. It turns out there was a set of twins in the grade right behind me. One of the twins was a big Beatles fan, and she found out that I had a ticket and that I was looking for somebody to go with. So she and I drove up to the concert. The tickets we had were way up there in the nosebleed section. And in the course of the day, while we were waiting for the concert to begin, we were in a restaurant getting a little bite of lunch.

And we struck up a conversation with these guys who were there for the concert from the University of Virginia at Charlesville. And their tickets were better than our tickets, a fair amount closer. So we started talking to them about the possibility of trading tickets. I don't think they really cared about seeing the Beatles, I think they were just there on a lark or something. So we each gave them ten or fifteen dollars, and our tickets, and they gave us their tickets. And that put us quite a bit closer than we would have been.

So we were on the side, I don't know how many rows up, but we had fairly decent seats. So the concert begins, and there was just an interminable number of other acts prior to the Beatles coming on. I only remember Clarence Frogman Henry, who was on just before the Beatles. And I really felt sorry for all of those opening acts, because nobody wanted to see anybody but the Beatles. And by the time poor Clarence was performing, people were really getting antsy, starting to bang on the seats. So Clarence finally exits the stage, and it's a fever pitch in there. And I'm sitting there saying to my friend, "You know, I hope for Pete's sake when they come out, people will not just scream and go absolutely bonkers, because I want to be able to hear them." I really did say that, believe it or not. So, just the way Ed Sullivan said, "Ladies and gentlemen, THE BEATLES!" whoever was the announcer said it almost exactly the same way. And sure enough, here they come, running out from the side. Well—I leapt out of my seat, I don't know how many feet up in the air, and screamed my head off. I mean, screamed like a banshee. I just totally forgot everything I had just been saying the minute before about "I certainly hope people act responsibly and maturely." I just screamed, I could not help it. It was like I had no control over myself whatsoever. I really and truly had been genuinely sincere just a minute before. Well, forget it. The minute they came out, you lost all sense of—anything, all control. You were just given over to the experience. And we had binoculars. And one by one, I went to each one, following them. To tell you the truth, you couldn't hear! You could not hear them playing, you could barely tell what song they were playing because it was just so loud in there.

And I've often thought about it over the years, and I think I heard them say one time, toward the end of touring, that it was very frustrating for them, because they really did care about the music, and they were doing their best to perform and improve as musicians, to improve as singers, to improve as a group, individually and collectively. They really did care about the music, but no one else did at the concerts. It was all about the experience of seeing them in person. But oh, my gosh, that was the highlight. We had to drive home that night 'cause the concert was a Sunday, and we had to go to school the next day.

And I remember coming into the school in the morning. I just could not wait to get to school to start telling people about this unbelievable experience that I had. To this day, when people learn that I was one of the people that actually saw the Beatles in person, they're always so impressed. Because, in the big scheme of things, over all these 40 years, since they didn't tour that much, there are not that many people out of the entire population of the United States that actually saw them in person.

* * *

The Beatles continued the tour with four more concerts in as many days:

September 14th Pittsburgh—Civic Center
September 15th Cleveland—Public Auditorium
September 16th New Orleans—City Park Stadium
September 17th Kansas City—Municipal Stadium

* * *

Charles Pfeiffer: In '64 they came to Kansas City. There's the famous story of Charles O. Findlay—they had bypassed Kansas City, it wasn't the biggest metropolis, and they were out in Denver, and Findlay, who owned the Kansas City Athletics said, "I'm going to get the Beatles to play Kansas City." He got a hold of Brian Epstein and offered him $50,000 and they said, "No, we're too tired." Then he offered them $100,000, they refused it, then he offered them $150,000 and they took him up on it, 'cause that was a fortune at the time for one concert. And they came out to Kansas City municipal stadium.

My best friend's mother bought tickets for him, his sister, her, and myself. I actually had the ticket in my hand. Right before the concert, my mother and I got into it over some little thing, and she said, "Well, you just won't go to the Beatle concert." And to this day I still give my mother a hard time about that. They took another kid in my place.

* * *

September 18th—Dallas-Memorial Coliseum

* * *

Carolyn Long Paulk: My friend Joy and I went to see them at Memorial Auditorium in Dallas on September 18th, 1964, and I got a program that I still have. Everybody was screaming, including us. And of course the amps were the size of our coffee table back then, so you really couldn't hear anything. And the same auditorium that looked so big back then was where my daughter graduated from high school in '94. In 1964 it was the biggest place in Dallas.

And the Beatles stayed at the Cabana Hotel. We wanted to go there but we were dependent on our moms to take us and pick us up. They wouldn't take us by there. So, the local radio station, KLIF 1190, had this sweepstakes going on—the Cabana hotel, which now is a jail—they were selling pieces of carpet from the room where the Beatles stayed for five bucks each. They were little two-inch squares. Well, I got one, and I've saved it all these years, and was showing it to one of my friends a few years ago. She said, "How do you know it came from there? It could be anybody's carpet from anywhere! And you paid five bucks for it?" And back then, that was big bucks. I just wanted something of them that I could have.

Everybody was standing up and screaming and crying, and we all had our favorites. John was always my favorite, but at that concert I was in my Paul phase.

* * *

This Dallas stop was the last stadium concert for the Beatles on the '64 tour. However, upon their return to New York on the 20th, they had one final performance scheduled, a cerebral palsy charity concert at the Paramount Theatre in Times Square. Tickets sold for up to one hundred dollars each, and the group played for no fee.

* * *

Carol Moore: When we got tickets, we got the last row of the theatre. We were at the very, very top. We were just lucky enough when we mailed for our tickets to get the last tickets. About a half an hour before the show we were sort of bored and noticed some sort of hallway. So we decided to go down the hallway and down some stairs. As we got to this one stairway, a guard caught us. So my sister and I ran one way, and ended up back of the lobby, so we can get back in. But the other girls went *down* the stairway and ended up in the Beatles' dressing room! And they saw a couple of Beatles before they got chased away. They came back and told us. They were quite hysterical. And one of the things I regret in my life was, why didn't I go down those stairs? I think about it from time to time when I'm having decisions in my life—should I take the more conservative or more aggressive route—and I think of the stairs and I think, "I oughta go down those stairs!" 'Cause I don't know what I'd miss if I don't.

Program for the cerebral palsy benefit concert at the Paramount in New York.

* * *

The Beatles left New York the day after the Paramount concert to return to London.

Once the group was back in England, it behooved observers of American popular culture to explain what had just occurred throughout the country in the preceding month. The reaction to the Beatles by teenage girls (and a good number of boys) whenever they found themselves either in the actual presence of the group, in close proximity, or even catching sight of their image on film or on television, is the stuff of legend. There was screaming. There was crying. There was fainting. These were very real, visceral, physical reactions to the Beatles. It's a compelling scenario, prompting explanations as to what it was about the group that actually triggered the intensity of these reactions. Authors and psychologists have for years postulated on the root causes of the madness.

Leave it to those who were there, who actually did the screaming, crying, and fainting, and who know from their own experiences and those of their contemporaries just why all of this happened the way it did:

* * *

Barbara Allen: I think a lot of it was a mass kind of hysteria took over in the way that a crowd reaction takes over. People get very excited—they're always searching, even at that age, for something exciting to break the tedium. And this was so new and different. And it came after the President's death, a very sad time that November, and that was still hanging heavy in the air. And all of a sudden, there were these young, vibrant men from a different country who were really cute . . . and I'm not a child psychologist, but we were young girls at an age where young girls start to have boyfriend fantasies. And because back then young girls were so sheltered , incredibly sheltered—not cloistered, we didn't go to Catholic school in my family—but we were very sheltered, protected, naïve, so this was a very safe thing. All of this early attraction to boys was played out safely with these kind of "boyfriend Beatles." Everybody had their favorite Beatle. For me, it was Ringo. So that became a "boyfriend" for these young girls who were starting to have these feelings toward the opposite sex but weren't able to express them. It was safe. It was OK for the parents—this is innocent, "they just have a photo of the guy, nothing's going to happen." I think that played

Suzanne Milstead and Barbara Allen clutch pictures of their favorite Beatles.

a role. And they were attractive looking as well.

I think people began to analyze that because adults, who were in the position to make social commentary, started to talk about that. Because these were not five-year-old kids in kindergarten—these were young women. Given the time period—you go back to the mid-'60s, you hadn't had all this revolution at that point. All the moms were at home, basically, the fathers went to work, and you didn't have all that liberation in all of its facets occurring yet. It was still like the old TV sitcoms—all of that lifestyle still was in gear. It was before Vietnam, before all of the disillusionment. . . . It was so different and safe and great back then. It really was.

Ilona Gabriel: A lot of people from that time, including my father who came from Europe, thought this was absolutely disgusting. Here were these four men with this long hair, standing onstage singing like that—that was an abomination. He even got the idea that maybe it was because we were just pre-teens and the hormones were going, he thought even at that time that it was more of a sexual thing, and it never was. At 12, that's something that I never thought about. But that was one of the things that *he* thought. So he was always afraid that by following the Beatles, I was going to be corrupted, and I was going to do things that I shouldn't do.

Carol Moore: I think what happened with a lot of young girls at the time was—before then, there was this whole thing growing up in the '50s about being the "good girl," the reserved girl, and not getting too excited in public. And the Beatles just broke our inhibitions, I think much more than Elvis, partially because the whole baby-boom generation was so much bigger, and then there were four Beatles. So it really did have a big psychological effect. And then of course, everything happened after that, in the '60s.

* * *

With so many millions of teenagers smitten with the Fab Four, it was inevitable that casual acquaintances, and even perfect strangers, would begin to bond with one another via their shared obsession with the Beatles. And all that was needed for a Beatles party was a basement, a portable record player, and a stack of Beatles 45s sporting the Capitol Records' famous yellow-and-orange swirl label.

* * *

Barbara Allen: In the spring, after all this insanity—it just reached this fever pitch—they announced that the group would be in Philadelphia on September 2nd for this concert. And that started up a whole new thing because by now a lot of the people you didn't know—this cemented friendships with girls you normally would not have known—you know how cliques are in high school, girls are funny that way. But this was a common thread that bound people together that normally weren't traveling in the same social circles. That was really interesting, how friendships grew out of this love of the Beatles.

Janet Lessard: I think the best part of this—when I wrote that article I was going into my first year at Bishop Fenwick high school. Some of the kids recognized my name, and there was girl there who had just come over from Poland, who could barely speak English, and she was somewhat ostracized because she just didn't fit into the norm because of the language barrier, and her appearance, she was just very different. But she immediately knew who the Beatles were, and at that time we didn't have MTV, we didn't have computers, we had the radio—and maybe once or twice a year you might see *The Ed Sullivan Show.* We weren't able to read a lot about the people we liked to listen to. We were kind of relegated to a radio at that point. So she came over and introduced herself in halting English, and told me her name and said, "Were you really at the concert? Did you really get to see them?" And we struck up a friendship, and to this day she's one of my best friends. We stayed friends from that point on, and I don't think she ever would have approached me except for this common bond that we had: the Beatles. So that's one of the things I remember from that time that I'm happy about.

Barbara Allen: After that, they started to have little parties. My friend Patty had a party in her home, in the basement, and they played Beatles music the whole time, and this was a new turn of events. Whereas in the past you'd play all the different artists, this was a real Beatles party. She had somehow gotten one of the albums—all Beatles music.

And the boys who were invited were starting to wear their hair longer, and they were getting involved in this whole thing. And that was good for us, because we *wanted* them to look like the Beatles! And through that party I met Sandy, and my friend Suzanne was already along, and she met the two girls through me. So the four of us became fast friends because of this interest in the group. And it bordered on obsession, I have to say. It was all we talked about, all we thought about 24 hours a day. It was always there.

Harold Montgomery: In those days, very rarely was there a person who liked two major bands. Especially in early '64, you didn't like the Beatles *and* Herman's Hermits. You can only like one. The fans were vicious! If you had a Herman's Hermits record, oh my God, they'd bitch at you. I was a big Beatles fan, all the girls knew it—it was kind of a girl magnet too. If you were a guy and liked the Beatles, the girls liked you. A lot of the guys thought that they were just a girls group, so they didn't like them, or they wouldn't admit it. They were more into the Beach Boys, or the Kingsmen, whatever. So being a guy and Beatles fan was being a little bit of a girl magnet, 'cause they could talk to you about it. But that's *all* they would talk about!

My mother actually bought "Mrs. Brown, You've Got a Lovely Daughter." And I liked the song, but I didn't actually like Herman's Hermits. Now, this was in 1964, and I went to a party and brought all of my Beatles 45s like everybody else did. That song was in there, and people got really, like, "What's *this*? What's this doing in there?" And you could not talk about other bands. You were dedicated, and that's it.

JoAnne McCormack: They were my entire life from the time I was 13 until 19 or 20. When I went to parties, if they didn't have Beatles records playing, I was outta there. It had to be Beatles and nothing but.

Harold Montgomery: Getting a single with a B-side not on any album was like we had found the Holy Grail. Just to have another track was amazing. I had a pen pal in England, and I had read somewhere that the Beatles' new album was coming out in America, but it was already out in England. So I asked him if we could trade for that album, so he sent me *Beatles for Sale*. And it had extra tracks on it. I went to a party and it brought it and said look what I've got, and took it out of a bag, and everybody loved the pictures of them. I was the hit of the party. The kids went ballistic 'cause it had two or three tracks on it that weren't on the American albums. We played it over, and over, and over again. People wanted to make sure they knew the tunes because they didn't know when they were ever going to hear them again. They were releasing songs in England and Europe that aren't going to come out over here—that was our scare. Until I got *Beatles for Sale,* I had no idea. We didn't get imports back then. English Beatles fans became great pen pals!

Maggie Welch: I had three girlfriends, and of course each of us had a different favorite Beatle. And, as luck might have it, we each resembled our favorite Beatle at least close enough to be more or less convincing, and we'd go around and do free little gigs. And we were even invited to perform on this local teen show, and we performed there, and we'd be called in for all sorts of little church events, teen dances, that kind of thing. And we just had a blast, because when we were doing that, we believed one hundred percent, you know, "I *was* John Lennon!" And Danielle *was* Paul McCartney! It was really fun. And we used to go downtown all the time, and tell people we were from England, using a British accent, that we lived on Henley-on-Thames, which we really didn't know where it was, but we got lots of mileage out of that. People would give us free things—just a typical adolescent prank. We made, as best we could, suits that looked like the Beatles'.

* * *

The Beatles' popularity among the original generation of baby boomers allowed for an avalanche of Beatles merchandise to beckon teens regardless of their budgets. Brian Epstein kept a loose reign on the array of products allowed to carry the Beatles' name and likeness, including socks, dolls, board games, talcum powder, harmonicas, and just about anything else that could fit into a shopping bag. Fans would trade with each other for sought-after items, and a few far-sighted fans even put away their cherished Beatles souvenirs for safe keeping.

* * *

Janet Lessard: From 1964 to '66, I collected everything that you could possibly collect. You've heard of the Beatles bobble-head dolls? I had all four of them. The lunch boxes. The shampoo. Everything. All of the albums that they ever released in Britain, because I had pen pals who would send me the albums.

And when I left home at 19, I just chucked them all. When I was 19, I married early, so I was more involved in that—leaving home and setting up my own place. Once I got into high school, there's more things to distract you from that.

Charles Pfeiffer: First I went out and started collecting all of the memorabilia. I had a Beatle wig—I got kicked out of school for wearing it in the school one day.

I wish I had all of the things I'd kept. Soon as they would release any single, any album, even the old stuff, like "My Bonnie" that they played with Tony Sheridan, I bought all the first releases of anything they had. . . . I have a fairly good collection still: the Beatle bubblegum cards, all those type of things. I studied them as much as I could, anything that came out about them, I'd read about it, I was just so intrigued by them.

Barbara Allen: And once they'd come here and there was all this press about them, the next phase for the girls was to go out and buy all this stuff—the trinkets, the Beatle buttons, magazines. They started to put out all of these Beatle magazines, and my friend Suzanne remembers making her father drive her out in a snowstorm blizzard to buy a Beatle magazine. That's how fanatical we became.

I found the Beatle pin that I saved. I have a pin that probably dates to 1964 with their faces, they're wearing their early Beatle suits—I think it's worth some money. I've never parted with it. I've kept it thinking it just feels right to hold onto it.

Harold Montgomery: Guys were really happy that there were buttons that said "I Like the Beatles" instead of "I Love the Beatles." A lot of boys didn't want to wear anything that said "love" on it, so that button was quite a find. They could wear it and not be considered a sissy!

Paula Lewis: I did start buying the magazines. I don't remember how or where they were sold, but I collected the trading cards. They were wonderful, and I had hundreds of them. Unfortunately, there was a house fire, and I lost a lot of things that I had, and the cards were among them. And I've grieved about those cards many times over the years.

Ilona Gabriel: You just couldn't have enough stuff. You couldn't have enough things on the wall in your room and on every schoolbook. The way you dressed changed, the way you wore your hair, just everything about you changed. Even the way you thought about things, because now all of a sudden you're hearing about the Beatles' opinions, and you don't really form your own. You're saying, "Yeah, that's true," and you kind of go along with it.

Dale Ford: I started buying every record that was out, in order of when it was released. I spent my whole allowance on that! I didn't have a lot of money to spend, but every penny I had went towards Beatles records.

Charles Pfeiffer: I still have some of the original 45 jackets, and I had them appraised. It's amazing how the jackets are worth more than the records, cause we'd all take the records and throw away the jackets.

Paula Myers: We bought all of their records, as many magazines as we could afford that had anything about the Beatles. We covered our bedroom walls with pictures. We had some in the bathroom, even under the toilet lid. We joined the Beatles fan club. We were in for the long haul.

Paula Myers and her favorite Beatles records, 1964.

Debbie Levitt: My house is what it is, I've kept every single article. My collection is so vast because I bought everything in twos and threes—one to play with, so to speak, one to look at, and one to keep.

I have a scrapbook of every article pertaining to the Beatles that I could find and cut out.

Do you realize I'm only up to '66 and I haven't finished it yet? If I was incarcerated and had nothing to do, I could finish it in a year.

I can tell you the catalogue number, the b-side, when it was released, that's the way I have my Beatle collection in my head.

Valerie Volponi: We cut out every article there was, and I did have a scrapbook of articles I clipped out of magazines and the newspaper. I used a lot of Scotch tape and glue, and I remember positioning the articles and cutting out their pictures—every page was special and had a special heading to it. I had several books like that. I just kept going, probably for two years.

Janet Lessard: I had a correspondence with about 10 girls in England, pen pals. And they would send me things—different magazine articles, new albums, and one girl sent me what she said was John Lennon's locks of hair. There was what looked like a certification from a hotel. It probably was as fake as could be, I really couldn't tell. Of course, we wanted to believe. That got thrown out too with all the bobble head dolls and lunchboxes, and all the other things I could sell on eBay and retire early.

Betty Taucher: The only Remco doll I have is Paul. My grandmother bought it for me at the World's Fair in New York, at the Japanese Pavilion. They were selling the dolls and she said "You can have one" and I think they were something like three dollars at the time. So I bought Paul, and I still have it.

Probably my favorite possession is: when John died—I write poetry, which I teach in school—I wrote about John and I sent it to Yoko, and she sent me one of his drawings back, with "Love, Yoko and Sean." I have two of them, in fact. She sent me another one later. And those are my two favorite things, apart from the program from the concert. And I have the tickets, scrapbooks of pictures . . .

I have some magazines in their original state, but not a lot, because what my girlfriends and I used to do, to afford all of the magazines that were Beatle-related, would pool our resources—and then get home and we would divide up all the pictures. And that way we'd all have something. Because there were so many then you couldn't keep up with it.

Carol Cox: I had to have it all, everything I could get my hands on. I wish I still had it. My mom made me throw it all out. I had the dolls in the boxes, the cards . . . I wanted everything I could get my hands on.

Paula Myers: I still have a lot of magazines and publications about the Beatles. Some are getting a little dog-eared, some are fading a bit. I have smaller things, like the Beatles guitar pin, trading cards. Mostly we spent our money on records and magazines. We didn't have a whole lot of money to spend, 'cause there were five kids in our family, and I kind of wish we had bought more. We also had scrapbooks that we put together. But we still have a lot of magazines that are still intact. I also have newsletters from the radio stations about the concerts at the Cow Palace.

Carol Moore: My sister and I both bought the magazines, and both kept scrapbooks, so we used to fight over the articles. I guess I got to the newspapers faster because my scrapbook's a lot thicker—or else I spent more money on the magazines.

Linda Cooper: After I got out of school, three of us picked up and got work permits and went to London. We loved the Beatles and we wanted to go to England. So we went there. While I was gone my mother sold our house and got rid of all my stuff. All my albums—I had so much stuff that I collected, and she just got rid of it!

Harold Montgomery: I have all my original stuff. My mother was so good, she never threw any of it out. I had everything. There was stuff that I never knew about that existed, and later on I got them through my trades or buying them at Beatlefests or stuff like that. When I lived back in New England, I had probably one of the largest collections of Beatles memorabilia. I remember going to Beatlefest in New York City, and John Ritter was looking for a Beatles record player. And I had one, and he gave me his card and said if I ever wanted to sell it to let him know. He was a huge Beatles fan.

Barbara Boggiano: I had to go out and get the John Lennon hat. As a matter of fact I still have it, and gave it to my daughter, 'cause my daughter loves John Lennon. I still have a lot of the memorabilia. I've got my Paul McCartney doll, and this little Beatle mophead thing that my penpal in Liverpool sent me. I still have it all on my little collector shelf. I had gotten *In His Own Write* on my 16th birthday, in 1966, and unfortunately I loaned it to a girl in high school and never got it back.

* * *

For the Beatles follow-up to their film debut, *A Hard Day's Night*, Richard Lester once again took the reigns as director, but decided to go in a different direction. *Help!* (originally titled *Eight Arms to Hold You*), was to have a different look and feel. There was more of a storyline in *Help!*, albeit a rather silly one, and the film benefited from being shot in color. Exotic locales such as the Bahamas and the Swiss Alps provided backdrops to a frantic chase involving a sacred ring that happens to get stuck on Ringo's finger.

Filming began in late February of '65 and continued into May, with the Beatles simultaneously recording their songs for the accompanying album.

While the Beatles continued to come up with perfectly crafted pop songs at an almost frightening rate, the *Help!* album already began to display signs of an ongoing maturity in their songwriting. John's title song, as well as his "You've Got to Hide Your Love Away," were his most personal and introspective songs to date, alongside his classic rocker "Ticket to Ride." Paul contributed gems such as "Another Girl" and, of course, "Yesterday," which was almost instantly destined to become one of the most covered songs of all time. George, for the first time, contributed two songs to an album, "I Need You" and "Tell Me What You See." Ringo handled the vocals on Carl Perkins' "Honey Don't." On June 11th, the Queen's Birthday Honors list was announced, and included the Beatles among the newest recipients of the title MBE (Member of the British Empire). The choice proved both popular and controversial, as several long-time holders of the title—mostly military veterans—protested the act of awarding the title to a group of mop-top musicians. To millions of Beatles fans, however, the royal honor served to validate their devotion to the group, as it recognized the cultural impact the Beatles had made in the U.K. in just two years.

Help! premiered in Britain on August 1st, and in various cities around the U.S. over the following few weeks, just before the group's return for their new tour. The fans, predictably, loved it—the critics liked it, but were not as enthralled with *Help!* as they had been with *A Hard Day's Night*.

* * *

Cathy McCoy-Morgan: I think my favorite album is the *Help!* album. It could be because when I was about 14 I got a job working here in Lansdale at the Music Hall Theatre, which is no longer there. I was working at the candy counter and *Help!* was playing there at the time. So I got to see it over and over again. I've probably seen it 50 times.

CHAPTER FIVE

The Shea Stadium Concert/1965 Tour

The Beatles returned to New York on August 14th to begin their '65 tour. For this latest visit to the Big Apple, they stayed at the Warwick Hotel on 54th St. and 6th Avenue (a.k.a. Avenue of the Americas). The Governor's Suite on the 33rd floor served as their accommodations.

In anticipation of their arrival, with over 100 policemen struggling to keep over 1,500 fans from swarming all over the group's motorcade, a plan was needed to avoid total chaos. The solution was to avoid the crushing hordes of screaming fans by bringing the motorcade west for one block on the eastbound 54th Street, thus allowing the famed passengers to scamper into the hotel before the outwitted fans on the opposite corner could catch up to them. The plan worked, but a near-riot still ensued at the hotel entrance seconds after the Beatles made their dash to the door.

* * *

Valerie Volponi: My friend Inga said, "Let's go down this street," and I said, "No, no, that's a one-way, they can't be coming that way." And she wanted to go down that street so that we could get a glimpse of them coming in. Well as it turns out, she was right. They did come the wrong way down the one-way street. She was mad at me for that!

* * *

By the day of the concert, however, the unshakable presence of the police and their barricades discouraged the crowds from remaining outside the hotel in full force, as they had on the day of the group's arrival. Some still remained, determined to get as close to the Beatles as possible, figuring that actually getting inside their hotel was half the battle.

While some sneaked in to hide in the hotel's various nooks & crannies, others tried a more straightforward approach: simply make a room reservation for the same day and hope to meet the Beatles as fellow guests of the hotel.

* * *

Kathy Albinder: My girlfriends Bernie, Lorraine and I had been at the Plaza the year before and we saw who got in. So it looked hopeless, but then we thought about it, and we did make reservations at least a month before. We heard from somebody that the Beatles were going to stay at the Warwick, but that wasn't the only place we made reservations. And we had gotten the confirmation back, so we had it for a long time. My friend Bernie had told her parents that she was gonna do that, so they told her no way are you going. So Lorraine got another friend.

We had confirmed reservations in writing. That's how we got through all the police and into the lobby. They didn't let anybody in, and we had seen that. We learned. So we got the confirmed reservations, and each of us had a little overnight bag, and we all got dressed up so we thought we'd look older. And we got into the lobby, and once they spotted us, they said they'd give us a room someplace else. But we said no, we don't want it. So we asked to talk to a manager, because we knew the Beatles were coming soon, and had landed at the airport.

But we did get to see them and I did get to talk to them for a minute or two. It was in the hotel lobby when they came in. And we were right there. There was no way the hotel was going to let us up there. But at least I got to see them up close, and we all thought they were so much better looking in person! And shorter. We were all wearing high heels, so that could have made a difference.

At least we got to see them, and that's all we really cared about. They kind of rushed through, and I think they were a little bit surprised to see us. But they were nice. Then they rushed upstairs, and we left. And that was the point. We only wanted to see them for a minute.

We went back into the crowd outside for a while. We were talking about it and everybody had heard about us. So everybody was talking to us, and the newspapers came over. It was the *Journal-American*, the *Daily News*, and my aunt had heard us interviewed on the radio. We were celebrities for 15 minutes, anyway. I called my aunt afterwards and I didn't remember saying this but my aunt Marie said that I said to her, "Now I can die, I've met the Beatles!"

We couldn't believe that nobody else thought of it. Because it was perfect. It worked out great! It was easier than we thought. It really was funny that we got through, especially with the police, cause they were tough on everybody. They weren't letting anybody through.

* * *

The Beatles' first order of business in New York was to return to the Ed Sullivan theatre to tape an appearance in front of a live audience, to be aired on Sullivan's season premiere broadcast the following month.

* * *

Annette Joseph Walker: For *The Ed Sullivan Show* in '64, I had one of those little brownie cameras, and tried to take pictures of the television screen. They came out, but you couldn't tell who it was or what it was. I was really upset about that, so I was hell bound and determined when I found out the next year that they were going to do the show again. I was going to get in there come hell or high water. The same group of six girls that I had met at Kennedy Airport, we exchanged phone numbers, so we were all banded together, and we'd call each other.

We had tried to go see them back in '64. We went out to Forest Hills stadium. That was a zoo. We went to the Paramount and couldn't get in there. And we just could not figure out how these people got these tickets. And it finally dawned on us that somebody was greasing some kind of wheels somewhere, and we had to do something. We went through a lot of stuff the first time, and we figured we had to be smarter Beatles fans the next go-round. We learned our lesson. We decided to make some plans this time. So we befriended one of the doormen at the backstage entrance of the Ed Sullivan Theatre. Every Saturday and Sunday, on our trips to Greenwich Village, we'd stop by there and say hello. And we got six tickets to a dress rehearsal from him. They had tickets for two dress rehearsals and one live taping. It was packed with young girls. The rehearsal we went to was 2:00 in the afternoon, or something like that. They were telling us that they wanted us to be quiet, which was ridiculous, and we couldn't take any photographs or bring in tape recorders. There just was no quiet. The Beatles couldn't hear themselves talk, so they'd have to walk off-stage. I was in hog heaven. We had made all of these plans to make sure we were in this audience. And to see it finally come to fruition was like, this is too good to be true! We talked to this guy, a very nice older gentleman. After that, we didn't stop seeing him 'cause we figured, hey, they may show up again!

* * *

New York promoter Sid Bernstein, who booked the group into Carnegie Hall the year before (for that prestigious venue's first true rock concert), found a way to top both his own and the Beatles' previous successes. He booked Shea Stadium for August 15th, where the group would play before a happily hysterical crowd of over 55,000, the largest ever for a rock concert at that time.

On that night, Beatlemania reached its delirious crescendo.

Shea Stadium was still sparkling new in the summer of '65, having been completed only the year before as the permanent home of the hapless New York Mets. The last-place team enjoyed a first-class stadium, with its façade memorably adorned with large, confetti-like sheets of multi-colored wavy metal squares. Immediately adjacent to the stadium at the time was, of course, the 1964–65 World's Fair, which had only two months left to go before closing forever.

Once Bernstein had announced that the Beatles would be playing Shea, his office was deluged with thousands of ticket requests, as were the other venues in the city selling the prized tickets. Incidentally, the highest ticket price for seeing the biggest rock group of all time: A whopping $5.65.

* * *

JoAnne McCormack: My girlfriend and I heard that they were selling tickets at the Cheetah Club in Manhattan, the closest place to us. I got up early in the morning and walked over to her house just as the

Ticket for the '65 Shea Stadium concert.

sun was coming up. We went in and stood on line and we got them. I ended up getting tickets for the last row in the loge. I said, "I am not staying here."

Kathy Albinder: Sid Bernstein got us tickets because my friend Bernie—the one who didn't show up because she told her parents—her father was friends with Sid Bernstein, and he had gotten us tickets, and we had really great seats. It was great. They were just wonderful.

Debbie Levitt: I have an older sister. And she happened to work for Sid Bernstein at the time. So when the tickets came around we naturally went and saw the show. I went to every Beatles show that there possibly was here—Carnegie Hall, Forest Hills, Atlantic City . . . and I have gone everywhere in this world to see them.

Linda Cooper: WWDC had a thing where they got so many odd tickets, and I had to do a lot of beg-borrow-and-stealing. I babysat and saved up the money. And they had a bus that went from D.C. up to New York. That was the year of the World's Fair. We went to the World's Fair and then we went to the show that night.

JoAnne McCormack: I remember the entire day, getting ready for the concert. It was sunny, it was really hot, and my cousin had come from Brooklyn to stay with me and go with me to the concert with my best friend across the street. And we all had our hair in curlers all day, we figured we had to look good. I wore a white pleated skirt and a sleeveless pink top with my Beatles pins, of course. . . . It was just great, the anticipation of the entire day—we couldn't eat, the three of us were together just giggling and carrying on, and my girlfriend's father brought us to Shea. You didn't eat a lot before the concert, 'cause you knew you were gonna be so excited, you didn't want to barf all over people.

Debbie Levitt: When you get on the train [to Shea] there was a sign that said "This train is taking you to see the Beatles." And the concert was just unbelievable. I figured who in this world is gonna come see this concert—I had seen them before that, but to see them in that kind of environment, in an open arena, with everybody else that we just bonded with.

* * *

Fans began to stream into Shea by late afternoon. The gates opened at 5:15, with about 5,000 fans rushing in. Hawkers made their rounds outside the stadium selling souvenirs. At the same time, the Beatles themselves were on a New York Air helicopter, taking off from the Wall St. helicopter pad, across the East River, and over to Queens. The original plan was to land on the grounds of the stadium itself, but they were not allowed to, and landed instead on the World's Fair pad. A Wells Fargo armored truck provided their transportation for the remaining few hundred yards to the stadium, where almost

57,000 adrenaline-fueled fans—mostly teenagers, mostly girls—awaited the Beatles' arrival.

With the stage set up squarely over second base on the diamond, and three rows of wooden barricades strung along the perimeter of the infield, the concert began at 8:00 P.M. with popular New York DJs Murray ("the K") Kaufman and Bruce ("Cousin Brucie") Morrow sharing MC duties. But the crowd's patience was to be severely tested before the main attraction. The warm-up acts included Sounds Incorporated (another band managed by Brian Epstein), the rather generically-named Discotheque Dancers, and singer Brenda Holloway, backed by King Curtis and his R&B band. Alas, the anticipatory screams for the Beatles drowned out the efforts of the opening acts.

* * *

Debbie Levitt: The warm-up acts were a tease. We didn't care who it was because half of the people didn't know who they were, it was like watching *Hullaballo* on TV but who cares—I'm sure at another venue at another time it would have been fine. But you're there to see the Beatles, not the go-go dancers, or have somebody come out and say "They're here, they're arriving, they're getting dressed" whatever. You could care less. The anticipation was nerve-wracking because anytime somebody came onstage to make an announcement, there was more screaming and yelling, and more anticipation, and someone would come out and it's not them.

JoAnne McCormack: I really didn't pay any attention until Ed Sullivan got on the stage. I could have cared less who was up there, it was like "Get this over with I wanna see the boys." And in those days, I think they came on about 9:00 and were gone by 9:45 [actually 9:30]. It was pretty quick.

Valerie Volponi: My friend Inga had an uncle who knew somebody who worked at Shea stadium, and offered to get us tickets. We had no idea until the day of the concert that our tickets were for the front row right behind the dugout. We couldn't believe how close we were. When the Beatles came out, we got to see the back of their heads really well! It was very overwhelming. You couldn't hear anything but a roar. And my cousin heard the roar. He lived several miles away and said you could hear it.

Debbie Levitt: When they finally introduced the Beatles, we didn't care if it was Murray the K or Cousin Brucie, we just didn't care. And when they took that stage, I honestly don't think anything's going to top that. For me it was more visual than a listening experience. I had seen them before that but here it's in the big arena, it's summertime, it's everything you want a summer experience to be. I never went to camp so this was my camp!

I actually sat down and wrote down on a paper I still have—the date, the time the concert started, the songs, I have it with the tickets. Everyone said, "What are you writing?" I said, "I'm paying attention, believe me!" Half the people didn't know what I was writing because they didn't know the songs.

* * *

Another of JoAnne McCormack's girlfriends had front row tickets on the field level by first base, thanks to yet another friend whose father was an usher at Shea.

* * *

JoAnne McCormack: During the concert I went down and tried to get in with them, but the usher there decided he was going to keep his row clear. So he sent me back. I certainly didn't go back up to the loge.

So now Ed Sullivan is introducing them and I said, "That's it, I don't care who said what." And I'm walking down and all the other aisles are choked with screaming girls, and this guy still thought he was going to keep his aisle clear, and as I'm walking down, he's got his hands crossed over his chest, shaking his head no, and Ed Sullivan says, "Here they are, the Beatles." And the tears rolled down my cheeks, he threw his hands up in the air, and that was it. I got to stay there with my girlfriends. He would have had to kill me to keep me from getting there at that point.

* * *

A quintessential scene of Beatlemania: JoAnne McCormack (center) having delirious fun in the stands of the legendary Shea Stadium concert.

McCormack even appears in several close-up cutaway shots of the front row crowds in the concert film shot by Sullivan's production company. Thirteen cameras, including one in a helicopter, were used to film the onstage activities and crowd reactions. It was first broadcast in the U.K. on March 1, 1966 (after a bit of audio dubbing by the group to improve upon their live stage performance), but was not aired in America until January 10, 1967.

* * *

JoAnne McCormack: I remember the camera being in my face, and it was like "Get out of the way! I can't see! You're blocking my view! John and Paul are up there, leave me alone!" It was just wild, it was absolutely wild. I wrote a list of the songs they played in the order they played them.

* * *

The songs played that night (and for most of the stops on the '65 tour) were: "Twist and Shout," "She's a Woman," "I Feel Fine," "Dizzy Miss Lizzy," "Ticket to Ride," "Everybody's Trying to Be My Baby," "Can't Buy Me Love," "Baby's in Black," "Act Naturally," "A Hard Day's Night," "Help!" and "I'm Down."

* * *

Ilona Gabriel: We had just turned 14, and my mother had to bring us to the subway. She went to the World's Fair while we were at the concert. It was hard to get a view of the stage, 'cause everyone stands up, but you could tell everything that was going on. We'd just focus on who our favorite Beatle was. We'd be nudging each other, "Did you see that, did you see the way he moved?" Things like that.

JoAnne McCormack: I could hear very little [of the music], a little bit here and there, because don't forget I was in the first row so the speakers were right in my face, but you'd just turn a little bit, you didn't hear a lot. Mostly what you heard was the screaming.

Kathy Albinder: The thing that stood out for me was the noise, because everybody was screaming, and nobody was really listening to them. Everybody was sort of watching them, and everybody kept saying, "Well, we don't have to listen to them because we have the records—we just want to see them!" I don't even remember if the equipment was any good that night, because you couldn't really tell and it really didn't make that much of a difference. It was just being there. And most people you want to see at a concert, you want to listen to what they're doing, but we didn't really care about what they were singing, 'cause we knew all the songs, it was just seeing them. All girls—there were a few guys around, and it was really fun. People were nice to each other. It was like a big cult experience.

Linda Cooper: John was acting so crazy! They were really kind of wired that night. It must have been from the crowd. They just seemed to be laughing a lot—in Baltimore, they came out, they were personable, but they just went through their repertoire. Here they were just kind of goofing off, waving more, and laughing, and playing off each other too. They looked like they were having a helluva good time. I just remember John on the organ, acting like his foot was stuck, and just acting kind of crazy. They were having as much fun as everybody else was. They seemed really psyched. I remember sitting and just being angry, like "Shut up! I want to hear!" I was crying but I wanted to hear! You couldn't hear diddly!

I think about those coats that they wore. They had to be roasting! I saw one of those jackets at Beatlefest, and was supposed to be the same material, and it was so heavy, I was thinking, "God, New York in August, they must have been dying!"

JoAnne McCormack: You're just so mesmerized by them that you're kind of in your own world, and you're not really aware of what's going on around you. I wasn't even aware of my girlfriend who was next to me. It was just like me and the Beatles. You don't do it consciously, but your body needs to take a break because you're just screaming and crying and just carrying on, and you're working at such a high level emotionally, and then your body just needs to come down a notch. And then, boom—you go right back up to the top level, and it's just kind of up and down like that, like an emotional roller coaster during the entire concert.

* * *

Murray the K, after performing his MC duties, retreated to the clubhouse under the stands and found, to his astonishment, dozens upon dozens of prostrate girls lying on every available flat surface, being attended to by the medical staff and police.

* * *

Linda Cooper: My friend Gloria and I went. And she, with the heat, and she was a screamer—she passed out. So then a policeman comes and hauls her off! And I'm thinking, "Oh my God. We have to get a bus, I'm how many hundreds of miles away from home, and there goes my girlfriend! What is my priority? I'm not leaving the concert!" I finally found her in some sort of tent that they had set up for all of the girls that had passed out.

Debbie Levitt: I went with my sister and I said, "How could you not be into it? Open your eyes, this is history! They're here!" And when you're looking, you don't know where to look first. Do you watch Ringo drum? Do you watch George? Do you watch Paul shake his head? If you had six pairs of eyes you wouldn't know where to look first. My sister just stood there, and she really doesn't have any memory of being there. I said, "Are you totally an ass? How could you not remember being there?" I close my eyes and I can see it. And everybody says that you couldn't hear any music. It wasn't just for the screaming, which it was, but you didn't even care what they were doing. It didn't matter what they were singing. Just to be enveloped in it, to be part of it, to take it all in. Of course they were so far out there. You just had to be there.

* * *

Also present in different sections of the stands were two young women who didn't know each other at the time, but whose lives would later intersect against truly astronomical odds. They were Linda Eastman, an aspiring rock photographer who, four years later, would become Mrs. Paul McCartney, and Barbara Goldbach, an aspiring model who would become known as actress Barbara Bach—and who, in 1981, became Mrs. Ringo Starr.

Upon the conclusion of the concert, the Beatles made a hasty exit in a white station wagon, $160,000 richer, leaving behind a stadium full of blubbering, crying, exhausted teenagers (of the $304,000 gross, promoter Sid Bernstein, after footing the bill for numerous expenses, took home a comparatively paltry $7,000).

* * *

JoAnne McCormack: It was totally emotionally and physically draining. You were so sweated up, it was a hot sticky summer night, you're jumping around like a crazy person. You were so exhausted, once they came off the stage you just sat there for a few minutes, and the tears just kept rolling down your face, and you didn't want to leave. We didn't have to get up right away because we were down in front and everyone else was milling out before us. We walked out emotionally and physically drained, looking for my girlfriend's father, and there are ten million people all over the place. Finally we found him and he took us home and it was just like "Wow!"

Barbara Boggiano: When I got to high school in September of '65, we were still very much caught up with what was happening.

When they did come to Shea Stadium, my mother just was not going to let us go. She said they didn't have the money for my sister and I to go. My girlfriend Susan and her sister Nanette, my best friends from school, were going. And there were eight kids in their family and only three in my family. And I was saying to my mother, "How can she go when there are eight kids in their family?" And my mother said, "Oh, her father works for the government." That was the end of that. And my sister and I would not talk to her for weeks. I was crying—I really felt bad for my father, because we were so upset that we could not go. And my girlfriends came back to tell us you couldn't hear anything, naturally, because of the screaming, and the Beatles were little tiny specks, she could barely see them. But it didn't really matter. To us, we were missing out on the experience of a lifetime. They were so fortunate that they were able to go. And of course, being part of the Beatles club, I found out who went, who didn't go—we had a weekly meeting, outside of the lockers, just to catch up on things.

Debbie Levitt: My parents were very supportive in anything that I did Beatle-wise. I have friends who say they regret their parents wouldn't let them go, and they still resent them. And I know a lot of people like that. But it was just something, it was just timing and place. I close my eyes and I absolutely see it. It was a beautiful night, it was perfect. And everybody threw away their tickets!

Debbie Levitt in her bedroom/Beatles shrine.

Maryanne Laffin: I went to the Shea Stadium concert by myself. None of my friends wanted to go. I saved up my baby-sitting money, gave it to my mother, she wrote me a check, I bought the ticket. My father dropped me off and picked me up. I remember coming home and I couldn't talk, I had such a sore throat!

* * *

Two months after the concert, on the day before the World's Fair closed, a time capsule constructed by Westinghouse was sealed and placed in the ground, designed to be opened in 5,000 years. There were 45 items placed inside the tube. One of those items was the 45 single of "A Hard Day's Night." So, it could be said that regardless of changing trends, styles of music, language, and cultural icons, evidence of the Beatles' contribution to our history is secure for at least the next 5,000 years. It would have been nice if the committee selecting the items would have thought to include a phonograph for playing the record. Instead, we'll have to hope the capsule will be opened by some very industrious people.

After the rousing Shea concert kicked off the tour, the Beatles spent the next five nights barnstorming the midwest from north to south to north again.

August 17th—Toronto—Maple Leaf Gardens
August 18th—Atlanta—Atlanta Stadium
August 19th—Houston—Sam Houston Coliseum
August 20th—Chicago—White Sox Park
August 21st—Minneapolis—Metropolitan Stadium

* * *

Wendi Tisland: I was from northern Minnesota, and my folks didn't have much money, so I cleaned the church to make money to go see the Beatles. My sister worked here so I took a bus down to Minneapolis by myself, and they took me out to the bus the next day, to the stadium. It was quite an experience. I got the tickets from WDGY, a mail in. I still have the ticket and envelope from WDGY, and the postage was four cents! I have my diary excerpt from seeing the concert, and also a big book of the tour. I got out to Metropolitan Stadium quite early, and everybody was trying to get a glimpse of the Beatles before the concert. We'd get crazy every time somebody moved down in the dugout area, we'd all be screaming and excited.

I remember when they came running out. It was quite a ways to run. It was the first real look and that was just a thrill of the night, when they first came out. Actually, it wasn't that wild, so you could hear the music. We were all excited, but it wasn't anything unruly or anything like that.

* * *

August 22nd—Portland, Oregon—Memorial Stadium
August 28th—San Diego—Balboa Stadium

On August 29th and 30th, the Beatles played the famed Hollywood Bowl in Los Angeles.

These concerts, plus another they performed the following year, were the only live Beatles concerts to be officially released as an album (in 1977). George Martin supervised the project, and, although the substandard audio quality posed a challenge, selected what he considered to be the best takes from the original tapes.

* * *

Paul Chasman: A friend of mine had a couple of tickets, and I went along—by the way, they were six bucks, which was a fortune in those days—I went just sort of as a lark, as much as anything else to watch the girls. But when they came out, I was caught up in it and I was as blown away as everybody else! I was just about jumping up and down and screaming myself. It really was an incredible phenomenon. I remember that I had never experienced music so powerful before. The power of their music really picked me up and transported me. At that age, it was quite stunning to experience something like that. All the girls were screaming and going nuts, but you could hear the music. They came out and started with John Lennon singing "Twist and Shout," and I was just out of my mind.

Up until that time, I liked all of their songs that came out. I liked them, and they were fine, but then after the concert, I really started to follow them, and started to realize with their progression with each album that they came out with, there was a growth and something new going on, and something exciting happening with each new release. So I think it was after the concert that I really started paying attention. And of course at that time—I started playing in bands when I was 13 years old, and the first band I was in was a surf band, and later got more into stuff like the Stones and the Beatles. I have to say the Stones' stuff was a lot easier to do than the Beatles'. The harmonies were really challenging, and I didn't know half the chords they were playing at that time.

* * *

The next stop was the Cow Palace in San Francisco for a concert on August 31st. Paula Myers had tickets, but found a way to see the Beatles earlier that day.

* * *

Paula Myers: My sister and I were trying to remember if we contacted a DJ at a radio station or if we contacted the company in charge of the concert production. I think it was a DJ. We heard about the press conference and wanted to try to get into it somehow. They said, "If you pass out fliers we'll send you to advertise the concert, we'll give you press passes." So we passed out the fliers, and when we got down there to get into the press conference, they said, "The press pass is only for one person." And my sister and I were inseparable. So we managed to talk them into letting both of us in.

They had kind of like a big fence up, and all these fans were outside, and boy did we feel like we were something else! Getting to go inside and all these fans outside wondering, "How did *they* get in?" We had an 8mm movie camera, so we just sat behind the press people. We took some movies which didn't come out all that well. The lighting wasn't very good for our camera, it was kind of dark.

You put someone up on a pedestal, and so when we saw them, we thought "They're actually like anybody else." They were being interviewed and John Lennon complained about the sound system at the concert before, how bad it was. John was the grumpier person, Paul was nicer. So they posed for pictures. They were sitting on the edge of a stage or table and were all swinging their legs together, kinda cute.

That night was the concert. They had added a concert earlier in the day, and the press conference was in between. My sister had really striking blonde hair, and John flirted with her, signaled to her or something, some kind of flirtation thing. So she thought that was really neat.

It was really exciting. We couldn't believe that we actually managed to pull it off. And the concert that evening was really loud, a lot of fans were rushing on the stage. And one girl grabbed John and John wasn't pleased at all. You could tell he was pretty angry, trying to shake her off.

Carol Cox: They were here in '64, and I wanted to go desperately. My dad said he sent for tickets and they sent a note back saying sorry, but they're all sold out. I cried and cried and cried. The next year, I didn't even have a hope.

We were at my cousin's house. And he said, "Carol, how would you like to go see the Beatles?" I started screaming! And he said, "You'll have to ask your mom and dad first." They were there, it was like a family dinner thing, and I'm going "Please, please, please!" My parents spoiled me rotten, so they gave in. What it turned out to be was my cousin through marriage had a brother who was a security guard, and he was going to be doing security work at the concert, and managed to get two tickets. And my cousin said, "You might get a chance to meet them after the show." So I came home and asked my girlfriend across the street to go with me. We were lucky because her sister and brother-in-law took us to the show.

I remember walking in there and walking farther and farther up into the stadium to the fourth row. We were fourth row on the end. Ahh!

And I remember my girlfriend said "If you scream, I'm gonna kill you," 'cause she knew I was a screamer. I don't remember who the first act was, maybe Brenda Holloway. I remember sitting there bored to tears, just waiting for the Beatles to come on. And I was doing this hand clap thing we used to do. And I looked up and she's imitating me. We just marked time until the Beatles came on. My girlfriend had the Instamatic camera, which at that time was brand new, with the flashcubes on it. I had a box camera, and had to pop the bulb out after every picture. Everybody was civilized until the Beatles came onstage. When the Beatles came out, it was mass chaos. I can't describe it any other way. It was like we were close to the stage until the Beatles came on and all of a sudden it felt like we were football fields away for some reason. Everything just erupted. It was real chaotic.

This guy came out of the audience on the right side of the stage, walked up to John, grabbed the hat off his head, and dove right into the audience in

Carol Cox's photos from the crowd at San Francisco's Cow Palace concert.

front of the stage. John mentioned it in the *Anthology*. It scared him half to death, and I can see why!

The overwhelming thing that I remember was standing there thinking they looked like they were on a screen. It was absolutely unreal to see them on the stage like that. Oh my God! My girlfriend kept saying, "Ringo's looking at me! Ringo's looking at me!" You're 12 or 13 years old and you want them to be looking at *you*.

We're actually the last generation to have seen them perform in concert and talk about it. Many years ago I found out the tickets weren't even really supposed to go to me. They were supposed to go to another cousin about my age who happened to be out of town that week, so that's why they came to me instead of him. I think it was fate! And when I talked to my cousin about five or six years ago, I said, "You know, that was one of the highlights of my life." And he said, "Then they went to the right person."

Dale Ford: I wanted to be in the elevated seats to avoid the fiasco of the first concert, where I had to get on my boyfriend's shoulders to look at them. For this, it was just me and my boyfriend's sister. She was maybe 12 at the time and I was 17 or 18 by then. We got elevated seats, but they were in the back of the Cow Palace, so we could see them the whole time, but they were tiny—we had binoculars but I didn't bother taking pictures. They started with "Twist and Shout" again, and I listened for it that time. They stayed on a little bit longer than the first time, they were a little more polished, they had a few new songs. And I stood up and started screaming and I guess she figured, well, if she can scream so can I! And the two of us just screamed through the whole thing, of course!

Paula Myers: After it was over, we went up to the stage. We had a program with us and we scrapped some of the dirt off the stage where they walked, and we smeared it in our program book. I still have that. We wanted something from them, even if it was dirt that they stepped on. We also sent away for a piece of a sheet that Paul had slept on.

Valerie Volponi: In September 1965, the Beatles were on their way back to England after their tour. This is from my diary:

> I kept my transistor radio with me at all times, since the local radio stations kept us abreast of all the Beatle activities, including the day the Beatles were flying back to England. On my way to high school one morning, I heard on the radio that they were leaving at 10:00 A.M. from Kennedy Airport. My sister Pam and my friend Inga immediately decided to skip school and go to the airport. Outside the school grounds, I gave my books to my cousin to hold, and we borrowed money from passing friends for the airport bus fare. We made made it to the airport and headed to the observation deck. We watched the Beatles walk from the terminal toward the jetliner, and as they climbed the stairs we yelled, Paul! George! Ringo! John!" They turned around, looked at us, and waved. We were thrilled beyond belief. Later that day, I confessed to my

mother that I had skipped school. I just had to see the Beatles. She understood and wrote an absence note for school.

I really like that memory.

* * *

Upon completing their '65 tour, the Beatles knew they needed to work on their second album of the year to be ready in time for Christmas. They spent October and November recording the songs that would be released as *Rubber Soul* in the first week of December.

Rubber Soul showed an unmistakable progression in the Beatles' music—from Paul's French-flavored ballad "Michelle," to the appearance of a sitar on "Norwegian Wood," to John's wistful introspection of "In My Life." These were clearly not the simple pop songs that had become so familiar on radio and in their concerts throughout the previous two years. *Rubber Soul* was the Beatles' major transition album, in which they demonstrated their uncanny ability to progress almost effortlessly away from bouncy pop songs to mature, sophisticated music that qualified as true art.

* * *

Art Murray: I loved music. And that superceded my attitude, frankly. It was hard for me to resist—the infectiousness of the music they made, which in any case was wall-to-wall on the radio, so you were not going to get away from it. And the profusion of Beatles hits, which for a long time were—I was attracted to them but at the same time they seemed kind of bubble-gummy, and not particularly impressive to me. That profusion probably lasted right through the end of my high school year, which was '65. And the Beatles by that time themselves had changed, but I'm not tracking that, frankly. What I'm hearing on the radio was probably a good six months to a year behind where the Beatles were, as a group, which I would not know until later. I wasn't really tuned into that at that point.

Linda Andriot: I saw them on *The Ed Sullivan Show*, like everybody else, and I didn't think too much of them at that point, because I was 11 years old, really young. I was really into baseball. So when I was 13, on November 9, 1965, I changed overnight from baseball to rock & roll, 'cause the guys in rock & roll are cuter! And I figured I might as well do what a teenager does and my sister was already watching the teen shows, and I started listening to WSAI back then. At Christmas time I asked for some Beatle albums, and I got *Rubber Soul,* and *Beatles '65.*

Linda Andriot's school photo.

January 4, 1966 was the day I fell in love with the Beatles. I remember thinking "Man, they are really good! They are really cool!" I was laying in bed thinking, "They're the best! I just love them!" It was in the evening of January 4th.

Linda Cooper: *Rubber Soul* is one of my absolute favorites. I love *Rubber Soul.*

Penny Wagner: *Rubber Soul* is my all-time favorite album.

Claire Krusch: *Rubber Soul* was probably the last album I ever got then. I wanted that for Christmas and I got it, and then I never bought Beatle albums again—until now. I buy all the CDs.

* * *

As thrilled as American record buyers were with the release of *Rubber Soul*, they were not really getting the true package, which had unfortunately become the norm by this point. As had been Capitol Records' practice from the beginning, songs were removed from the original British version of *Rubber Soul*, to be combined later with songs that had been released in Britain as singles, thus creating "extra" albums for the American market. So, in the case of *Rubber Soul*, the songs "Drive My Car," "Nowhere Man," "What Goes On?" and "If I Needed Someone" did not appear on the American release. They were put aside for inclusion on Capitol's *Yesterday and Today* LP, released about six months later. In their place, Capitol included "I've Just Seen a Face" and "It's Only Love," both originally released on the British *Help!* LP.

This practice became especially annoying with the *Rubber Soul* and *Revolver* albums because the Beatles had begun to make their albums complete, self-contained works of art, increasingly distinct from each other, both in packaging and in the music itself.

In June, Capitol released *Yesterday and Today*, comprised of the songs "Yesterday" and "Act Naturally" from the British *Help!* album, the four songs lifted from the British *Rubber Soul*, and the single "We Can Work It Out"/"Day Tripper." In addition, three songs from the upcoming British *Revolver* were also included: The brilliant "I'm Only Sleeping," "And Your Bird Can Sing," and "Dr. Robert"—all John Lennon compositions. The result is a mish-mash collection of songs (albeit brilliant ones) plucked from just about everywhere to give us the album *Yesterday and Today*. It would also later create a very lopsided American version of *Revolver*, to be released that August, but featuring only two Lennon songs, "She Said, She Said" and "Tomorrow Never Knows." At this point, most American fans were still unaware of how Beatles albums were being chopped up and rearranged by Capitol.

CHAPTER SIX

The 1966 Tour

The year 1966 brought not only still more staggering success both creatively and commercially for the Beatles, but also a few moments of very real crisis.

On June 23rd, they departed for Munich, Germany, to begin their next world tour. From there it was on to Tokyo (with an unscheduled stop in Anchorage, Alaska, due to a typhoon warning). In Tokyo, they performed two concerts at the famous Budokan martial arts hall, which were videotaped and broadcast on Japan-TV. Then it was off to Manila, Philippines, where they received the usual hysterical welcome by a crowd of thousands. So far, so good.

At one point during their brief stay in Manila, an invitation was sent to the Beatles to attend a luncheon in the presence of Imelda Marcos, wife of dictator Ferdinand Marcos (and, as the world would learn years later, owner of an infamous 3,000 pairs of shoes). The event did in fact conflict with the Beatles' schedule for that day, so the group simply gave it a miss, unaware that it would be seen as a snub to the country's First Lady and her family. Anger in the press and among Philippine citizens seemed to grow more bloodthirsty with each passing hour.

After the Beatles performed their two concerts, the rising hostility directed at them became frightening. They had every intention of leaving the country as quickly as possible, but were hampered by angry, shoving mobs at their hotel and at the airport, with security officers rendering little assistance. They were even delayed in taking off due to a last-minute bit of bureaucratic red tape cooked up by the government intended to hassle them even further before allowing them to leave. Brian Epstein and publicist Tony Barrow had to secure proper documents while the group waited nervously at the airport.

The ugly incident did not help the Beatles' already reluctant attitude towards touring, but things would get even worse in America a month later.

In the first week of August, *Datebook* magazine reprinted an interview with John conducted by Maureen Cleave several months earlier. During their talk, John made several comments about the Beatles' popularity among young people, and how "We're more popular than Jesus now." He also predicted the eventual end of Christianity. Once those comments were published in the U.S., just two weeks before the start of the American tour, all hell broke loose, especially in the Bible Belt, where radio stations adamantly refused to continue playing Beatles music, and even promoted public bonfires for burning all Beatles records and magazines. It looked as if the group was headed for disaster. Brian Epstein was so panicked he wondered whether or not he should cancel the entire tour. At the very least, he had to repeatedly reassure the American public via several press interviews that John's words had been taken out of context, and that he was merely expressing his concern over how Christianity seemed to be losing a significant role in the lives of young people.

* * *

Jim Rugino: When John said, "We're more popular than Jesus," I agreed. I was a Roman Catholic. I had been confirmed, I had taken Paul's name as my confirmation name. But when it came down to it, I was more into the Beatles than I was into the Church.

Carol Moore: I was Catholic, and I basically left the Church, and I always say that the Beatles were one reason. The other reason was because I read Ayn Rand, who was very anti-religion. And the Catholic Church and organized Christian religion just seemed so irrelevant to what was really going on. So when John later said "We're bigger than Jesus" and then explained what he meant and everything, I was saying, "Yeah, yeah! You know—they are part of some new, religious, spiritual experience." I did feel that very strongly.

* * *

The controversy of John's remarks overshadowed what should have been a triumphant event in the Beatles' career: The release of the *Revolver* LP in the first week of August.

Revolver not only continued the group's creative momentum, which shined so brightly on *Rubber Soul*, but expanded upon it and introduced new sounds and moods in ways no rock group had done before. From the opening track, George's "Taxman," to John's closing "Tomorrow Never Knows," the album is full of remarkable musical innovation and variety. "Eleanor Rigby" uses a string section behind Paul's vocal, much like the arrangement for "Yesterday." The lyrics throughout the album also mark a departure from the familiar songs of love won and/or lost. John's pristine "I'm Only Sleeping" experiments with backwards tape loops, as does his most jarring track to date, "Tomorrow Never Knows." (Just a reminder: In America, Capitol's version of *Revolver* omitted three outstanding Lennon songs that were put on the earlier release *Yesterday and Today*, so fans must have wondered if John was "only sleeping" during much of the *Revolver* sessions. In fact, it was arguably his most creative period.)

Ringo also chimes in with the sing-along "Yellow Submarine," and, for the first time, George makes three songwriting contributions to a Beatles album. "Love You To" is his first Indian-flavored song, and his first to feature a sitar. In short, *Revolver* set a still higher standard for the rock music world to meet.

It is telling, however, that the group never performed any songs from *Revolver* on their final tour (they did perform "Paperback Writer," which was recorded early in the *Revolver* sessions but released as a single). Their increasing use of new and innovative recording effects would have made it impossible for them to faithfully reproduce with only two guitars, a bass, and drums. This became one of several key reasons why the 1966 tour would be their last.

On August 11th, the Beatles began the tour with a flight from London to Chicago, stopping in Boston to switch planes. Once in Chicago, John himself faced the press to reiterate his regret over his controversial comments. Most Beatles fans accepted his explanation, regardless of its questionable sincerity. After all, at that time, considering the immense influence the Beatles had on millions of young people around the world, it was not such a stretch to consider them more popular than Jesus. But for the older generations, having a *Beatle* say so was seen as the height of arrogance and disrespect. Questions dogged John throughout the tour, and for the first time, the group experienced playing to crowds that fell far short of sell-out capacity.

The first concert of the tour took place on August 12th at Chicago's International Amphitheater. The next day the group played at Detroit's Olympia Stadium, and then continued on to Cleveland for a concert at Cleveland Stadium on the 14th.

* * *

Betty Taucher: There were two real popular radio stations in Cleveland, KYW and WHK, and we could also pull in CKLW out of Detroit, which was Motown, 'cause you didn't hear much Motown on the local stations. And KYW and WHK competed with each other, with DJs, the song lists, and WHK sponsored the Beatles coming here in '64.

By '66, another station had come on, WIXY, and they were an AM station also, and they kind of overshadowed the other two. They sponsored the Beatles coming to Cleveland Municipal Stadium on Sunday.

There was no Ticketmaster or anything like that then, so the only way to buy tickets was to go down to the stadium and sit in line. So my father was going to take us girls and sit with us for the night in line, 'cause he didn't want us going by ourselves, and my parents figured there was going to be no holding me back this time. So my mother said, "Fine, you can see them as long as I go." My father was all set to take us, and I had an aunt who was taking an art class taught by somebody who worked at WIXY. And he passed out tickets to everybody in the class. So she called my mother and said, "You wouldn't be interested in them would you?" So I got three tickets and didn't have to sit in line.

And then the day before [the concert] they stayed at the downtown Sheraton. And we were at my girlfriend's house. There were about a dozen of us girls, and of course we were all going to the concert the next day, and her mother called all of our mothers while we were at her house, on the pretext of swimming in her pool, and said, "We're going downtown." In those days there were no seatbelts, so you just piled in the car—all of us girls in the back seat, and we rode downtown, alternating spaces so nobody died. And Cheryl's mom dropped us off at the Sheraton and said, "Okay I'll be back in about three hours, you girls just have a good time." And there were like thousands of people out there, we were all screaming to get into the hotel. We tried to get in a million times. We got as far as the elevator, and got thrown out. We were dying 'cause we knew they were up there. It was just the thought that they might show up or somebody might come by, or just the feeling. There were things you'd do for them that you would never think of doing for anybody else. I like lots other groups but you wouldn't do that for them the way you would do it for the Beatles. The concert itself was only half an hour. Paul did most of the talking, which I think he generally did.

I remember the limousine coming onto the field, with the whole bunch of motorcycles. The stage was set diagonally, and nobody was sitting behind it [in the stands]. They only sold 25,000 tickets. The stadium could hold 80,000 people, but they only sold 25,000 because back then stadium concerts were a new and novel thing. Nobody thought stadium concerts were gonna work. They thought 25,000 was an enormous amount of people, so that was all they were allowing. So everyone was sort of at the farther end, facing them. The trailer that they stayed in was behind them.

* * *

Despite the controversies of the previous month, Beatlemania and its accompanying hysteria was not over just yet. At one point during the Cleveland concert, the crowd got out of control, as a mob of frantic fans rushed the stage, forcing a temporary halt to the show. The Beatles made a hasty exit back into the trailer for the half-hour interruption, during which police cleared the area in front of the stage of over-zealous girls, many of who lost their shoes in the rampage.

* * *

Betty Taucher: I was in the second tier of the stadium right in the front row, so I was happily draped over the wall, and my mother was just holding my feet. The people that were down on the first level—because the stadium being as old as it was, it was real easy to

Ticket for the Beatles' 1966 Cleveland concert.

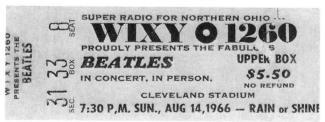

get on the field. You could just go right over the railing and get on the field. Well, all these people that were on the first level went over the railing and ran out onto the field. And most of them lost their shoes in the running. The next day in the paper the picture was of this huge pile of shoes, and the caption was "Beatle fans, here are your shoes."

There were no huge towers of sound equipment and stuff like there is now. Now you could have 100,000 fans screaming and you could still hear the concert. Then you only heard bits and pieces, but that wasn't the idea. We knew we weren't going to hear anything. It was the idea that you were there and they were there. You were in the same place with them, and you were close to them and could look out and see them. And that was the neat thing. They were just as energetic, just as much into it, they were really doing it for the fans. They cared a lot about the fans, which I think we felt.

The programs were a whole dollar, which nowadays seems insane. The tickets were $3.50 and $5.50 for the concert. And $5.50 was considered a high ticket price back then, considering what you'd pay for a movie or whatever. An album was only $2.98. A 45 you bought three for a dollar.

The trailer behind the stage was independently owned. The Beatles stayed in it while Cyrkle and Bobby Hebb played. And when the fans went onto the field, they went into the trailer for a while, while the police sent the fans back. The fans left their shoes in a heap and went back to their seats, and then the Beatles came out again.

I got to see the trailer after the concert. It was on exhibit at the County Fair. And the guy that owned the trailer didn't disturb anything at the time. The glasses still had all the fingerprints on it and stuff. So my girlfriend and I went and we just spent the whole day going in and out of it—I got to sit on Paul's bed, and hold his glass and touch his towel, and sit in his chair, and all that kind of stuff. It made you feel close to him, that you got to touch something that you knew just a couple of weeks before they had touched, you hadn't even washed it. You didn't care about that there might have been 10,000 people before who touched it, you were touching the same thing that he touched, and vicariously it was like being close to him. They charged a quarter. After we spent about a dollar, the cop that was guarding it just let us go in, "You two don't have to pay anymore just keep on going, I understand why you're here, just keep going, it's fine . . . "

They could have actually traveled in it. It had a kitchen, it had bedrooms, a bathroom, and you're like, "Whoa this is pretty neat" considering how trailers were in those days.

I didn't see it again until December of '81, when the owner put it up on display at the mall, and allowed people to go into it. It was in honor of John, the year after John had died.

* * *

August 15th Washington, D.C.—D.C. Stadium

* * *

Deborah McDermott: My parents got the tickets [for the Washington concert]. I remember begging and pleading, and I had a friend who was the same age, and the two of us were begging our parents. They only way they'd let me go was with my sister and a friend of hers. I still have the original program, and she still has the tickets.

Pete Kennedy: My mom drove us down to Waxie Maxie's, a record store where you'd go to get tickets for the big concerts. We went down the day the concert was announced. The tickets were for my sister and I—she was a year younger—and my older sister had to drive us to the show, since we were too young to drive. She was a folk fan who didn't really like the Beatles all that much. She was one of the fingers-in-the-ears people, enduring the shrill of screaming the whole time. But it was very nice of her to do that.

At the D.C. concert, the Beatles were staying at an exclusive hotel, the Shoreham, and no one knew what Cyrkle looked like. So these kids got the brilliant idea of going down to the Shoreham, calling a limo service saying they were Cyrkle, and renting a limo that would pick them up. And the limo driver took them to the backstage door of the stadium, and took them in, and they went down into the locker room. And they hung around for a while, and I think they actually did meet the Beatles. And they were fine until the actual Cyrkle showed up, and then they got thrown out. But those guys were legendary in D.C. after that.

The Remains came out and played some songs that nobody knew, and they stayed onstage when Bobby Hebb came out and sang "Sunny." Then Cyrkle got up and sang "Red Rubber Ball" and some other songs.

And then there was a long wait until the Ronettes came up. Then it seemed like an interminable wait.

And one of my favorite moments after waiting and waiting was Mal Evans—although at the time I didn't know it was Mal Evans—but this big guy with glasses on came out of the dugout carrying a Rickenbacher twelve-string and the extra Hofner bass. And at that moment, the whole place went crazy, but there were no Beatles yet! It was sort of like a proof that the Beatles were really there, in the same space as us. And I thought that was the coolest thing! It was the ultimate reality check, like this is really going to happen.

And when the Beatles came out it was just like a pandemonium. They had to walk from the dugout to the stage. And I noticed that they had cameras themselves, and as they walked out they were taking pictures—maybe realizing that this stadium thing wasn't going to go on forever. Then they finally got onstage. You could only hear the first few notes of each song, and then there was an enveloping white noise at about 130db that covered everything else up, and it was in waves. It would dip down a little bit at the end of the song, and it seemed like McCartney was kind of like the front man of the band. Lennon was kind of goofing around, Harrison was kind of staring off into space, and Ringo was just being Ringo. And McCartney was the one who was really communicating with the crowd, and he had amazing control of the crowd, just by jumping up and down or moving his bass or spinning around, 'cause he knew he could make the screams even louder. He had perfect timing. It was amazing stagecraft.

Deborah McDermott: Why did we scream? At the concert, it was absolutely group reaction. It was August, it was hot, it was sticky, as only D.C. can be in

August. The place was packed with kids my age. I went with my older sister, who is 10 years older than me and now wears it as a badge of honor that she saw the Beatles, but really had no interest in it back then. It was like we were all there for one reason, and we were there to idolize the Beatles. We were all 14, 15, 16 years old, and that meant screaming, and not really listening. I remember being borne away by all of the energy around me. It was the energy of all these like-minded teenagers around me, there for one purpose. And the energy was what drove all of us to yell and scream. I remember there was a cyclone fence that we were clawing, screaming their names.

Pete Kennedy: I noticed the only new song they did was "Paperback Writer." It sounded pretty raggedy because it was a studio creation, and was probably not a good idea to try it live, but they did it. It would have been hard to hear what they were doing even without all the screaming. But with the screaming it was a blanket of noise. And nobody was mad because it really was a cultural event, we all kind of knew that. You weren't listening carefully to the music; you were in the same place as the Beatles and you were with these other 40,000 people who were going through this transformative experience at the same time.

Deborah McDermott: At one point Paul said, "Please quiet down. I want to play something for you. This is new, and I want you to hear it." And there was hardly a discernable decibel change. And I became quiet, because I wanted to hear what it was. It was "Yesterday."

* * *

August 16th Philadelphia—JFK Stadium

* * *

Linda Cooper: My girlfriend and I got tickets and saw them at JFK in August of '66.

I did notice that sometimes, if you could even attempt to hear some of the songs, that they didn't sing the same words. I asked Sharon, "Do you think they're doing that just to see if people are paying attention?" I can't remember what song it was, but they're singing along and you know every bloody word, and it's a totally different word, and I'm like, "Now why did they do that?" But I didn't see anything lackluster.

Ticket to the '66 Philadelphia concert.

It got so insane and I think they could have toured more if it hadn't been so restrictive. I can't even imagine just being around some of the places they were, and to see the insanity, I can imagine that you couldn't do anything. It would be really awful I would think.

Cathy McCoy-Morgan's original desk calendar from August 1966, with a very special concert date circled.

Cathy McCoy-Morgan: They had them in the middle of the football field, and we were back in the bleachers. We couldn't really see them or hear them very well but it was just being there that was so wonderful. And the mania—everybody was feeling that.

And it was so cute when we got back to the Reading terminal, the people who were announcing what train was coming next were saying things like "Paul McCartney please report to the . . . " just to get everybody in an uproar. But it was *fun*. It was just really great.

* * *

After an August 17th concert at Maple Leaf Gardens in Toronto, the Beatles moved on to the Boston area for their August 18th concert at Suffolk Downs Racetrack.

* * *

Harold Montgomery: I never thought I'd get to see them in concert and then, for my 16th birthday, my mother bought my cousin and I tickets. We were living in Springfield, Massachusetts at the time. She saw an ad in the newspaper, and it said there were two busses on the Peter Pan bus line—they were running a special to the Beatles concert, with chaperones. She got them for me as an early birthday gift, and I'm so glad she did, 'cause it was the last tour. But every year when they'd come and tour they'd never be anywhere near. I was too young to go to Boston by myself. She knew I was dedicated because I'd been hardcore for three years.

I remember every single step of the way. We had big banners on the sides of the bus, some kinds hung them from the windows. They said "Beatles or Bust" and we were all trading and reading magazines on the way. Everybody felt like they knew each other. You were immediately connected with all these kids. Everybody was instantly friends.

We got off the bus, we went through the gates, showed our tickets. They were selling all kinds of things. The concession stand was selling cookies with Beatle hair cuts on them. They were calling the lemonade "Lennon-aide." They had stacks of the *Boston Globe*—I still have the issue—and it said, "Beatles Plan Retirement." At least 50 percent of it was stories and pictures of them.

We went to our seats and decided we didn't like where we were sitting, so we decided we were going to start to see if we could get up closer. Nobody was onstage yet. It was just a stage with a wooden frame and wooden roof, right by the track, facing the grandstand. Every time a limousine pulled up, the screams were unbelievable. Anything that was pulling up near the stage, the screams were just incredible.

Bobby Hebb played "Sunny," but it was like a 15-minute version, much longer than the radio version. Then Cyrkle, the Remains, then the Ronettes, then the Beatles. The [other groups] weren't on for a long time. But when you wanted to just the see the Beatles, they were on too long!

They pushed all the stuff off the stage, and everyone was getting really antsy because it was taking so long to clear the stage. But once that Beatles drum kit went up on the podium, it was non-stop. It was just massive screaming. I got down to a fence by a speaker to the left of the stage. All of a sudden this limousine pulled up, and the place just went bonkers, but they weren't in it because they seemed to come out from the field where there was no car. I could see them walking towards the stage, but they weren't in that limousine. I think it was waiting for them to run into when they got off the stage. Once people knew it was them, the flash cubes were like lightning. It was amazing. It was very hypnotic.

They opened up with "Twist and Shout," "Baby's In Black," basically the same play list. They were laughing and you could hear them talking to each other, and they'd go up to the mike—and it was exactly like all the bootlegs you'd hear where they'd go, "Hello, hello! Can you hear us?" I only got to stay where I was for the first song, and then they told me I had to go back to my seat. I started heading that way but I didn't do it. It just got so nuts, they couldn't have moved everybody. By the second or

Suffolk Downs '66 concert from the stands.

third song, there was no way they could have gotten people standing in the aisles out of the way. It would have taken an army. They were just bonkers. I paid attention to it, I was aware of, what are the other guys doing? How are they getting excited? They were just hollering, not like the screams, just hollering and whistling. I couldn't believe I was seeing them live. I just couldn't believe it. And then it was over, and I just went, "Oh my God! That was so fast!" like it was 15 minutes long. There were girls crying, and hearing guys saying, "Oh, that was so cool! They were so tough!" That was the guy thing to say about them. There was a comraderie with the guys there. "Did you like it?" "Oh, they were tough!"

And the fans didn't want to leave. But we didn't want to miss our bus. It was just amazing. I sat in the bus, and I was kind of shaking, like I had just witnessed something historical, and I was still vibrating from it. Inside the bus everybody was bonkers. We were all singing the songs, standing up in the bus, certain groups were talking about this and that, showing things that we bought. I remember coming home after the concert. The whole bunch of us, maybe eight of us, got off at this one stop near my home. We were all singing, here it was close to midnight, and these cops came by and thought maybe we were drunk teenagers. We said, "No, we just got home from the Beatles!" And they said, "Okay, just everybody go home and be quiet." I haven't thought of that in years. As soon as we got in the house my mother asked, " So how was it?" And I said, "Oh, it was the best thing I have ever seen." And we bought this little felt banner that says "I Love You Beatles" and I tacked it right up on my wall and my mother said, "Let me take a picture of the two of you in front of it."

Harold Montgomery (right) and his cousin Paul moments after returning from the Suffolk Downs concert.

* * *

The next stop was the Mid-South Coliseum in Memphis on the 19th, after which the group was scheduled to play at Crosley Field in Cincinnati. Mother Nature had other plans, however, dousing the area with rain, and causing a last-minute postponement. The only solution to keep things on schedule was to play a Sunday double-header: Crosley Field in Cincinnati early Sunday afternoon, followed by the scheduled concert at Busch Stadium in St. Louis a few hours later.

* * *

Linda Andriot: I begged my parents for months to let me go. My parents weren't gonna let me go at all. And I was not happy about it. My dad was a policeman and he was in charge of the police detail. And that was August 20th on a Saturday, but it just rained and poured down. And I remember being at home and crying my eyes out, like "They won't let me go!" And my sister was more into Herman's Hermits. And I begged my parents to let me go, but they didn't play on that Saturday night, cause of the rain. And John Lennon said to somebody, "What are we doing tomorrow afternoon?" And they were doing St. Louis that evening, so they decided to play at Crosley Field that Sunday afternoon. My dad worked on Saturday from 3:00 to 11:00, and he'd double back on Sunday and worked from 7:00 to 3:00, so he was still in charge of the Beatles' traffic problems . . . so he called home and asked my mom, "Did the girls go to church?" And my mom said yeah, and he said, "Okay, I've got tickets for them, bring 'em down to Crosley Field." Somebody couldn't make it the next day 'cause they were out of town and just gave the tickets to him. A lot of people came from out of town and just couldn't spend the night, and they missed it.

So my sister and I ran into our rooms and changed our clothes as fast as we could, and out the door, in the car. I was just so excited. I remember riding down in the car, and the Beatles were being interviewed on the radio. It was really cool. We met my dad down there, we got a police escort into Crosley Field, my dad took us over to a policeman and said, "These are my daughters. When the show's over, they'll be sitting over there so take them back to the police station." My sister and I sat in our seats the entire time, never went to the bathroom, never went anywhere, we never saw the souvenirs of anything at all. But we were there. Everybody was just screaming. I remember seeing them, I remember just being so happy. I don't know if we heard them or not, because it was more like seeing them than anything. You could hear something, I'm sure. But I remember just being there and just watching it. Our seats were on the lower level, maybe 30 rows back. It was overwhelming. Put it this way: the Beatles couldn't do anything wrong. Each and every one of us was thrilled to be there.

And we got the police escort out of there and were taken to the police station. We had to wait for my dad to get off work, and I guess he got off work about 3:00.

My dad and this one guy came out and said, "The Beatles paddy wagon is back there if you want to go look at it." So we walked into the paddy wagon that the Beatles were transported in. And I touched the seats of the paddy wagon. Some policeman gave me a little tiny piece of the stage, about the size of a dime, that got lost somewhere along the way. But my dad asked the guy driving the paddy wagon to get Paul's autograph. And he did! And I have it on police stationery.

* * *

On August 23rd, the Beatles returned to Shea Stadium in New York for their second and final concert there. Annette Joseph Walker remembers how her attempt to get a ticket failed, causing her to lose hope of attending the show. She could never have dreamed what would happen in the last days before the concert.

* * *

Annette Joseph Walker: We'd spend Saturdays and Sundays hanging out in Washington Square Park in Greenwich Village, or sitting in one of the coffee shops. We met this older, rather disheveled gentleman who walked up to us one day as we're sitting in the park, and he just started talking to us, asking us about what kind of music we liked. Most weekends he'd show up sooner or later. He was never pushy or seemed to want anything from us, other than to talk to us. So we didn't see that he was any harm, so we talked to him. I remember we were all standing around, and apparently there was some order form that you could get to order the tickets for Shea. They'd let you know up front that just because you sent your money, you weren't guaranteed to get a ticket. I had sent the form in for two tickets. I got the form and money order back, but no tickets. One of my friends sent for two tickets and got just one.

So we're standing out there maybe a week or two before the concert, and I'm moaning and whining and complaining because I didn't get tickets. And the guy we talked to said, "Well, you can go to the concert too," and pulls out two tickets and gives them to me. He gave me the two tickets and his business card, and I was just speechless. He tells me, "If you have any problems, call me." We were all screaming and jumping up and down and carrying on, and he just kind of disappeared.

And it turns out he was Sid Bernstein. We had no clue who he was, or who Sid Bernstein was for that matter. It wasn't like he introduced himself or anything. We just called him the old guy. It was just a bunch of people standing around doing absolutely nothing, and he just walked up and said hi, just small talk at first, then talking about music, and he seemed very knowledgeable about music.

When I showed the tickets to my mother, she decides I wasn't going. She said she had seen that madness on TV, and I did not need to be a part of it. So I talked to her and talked to her. And I showed her that I had mailed in money for the tickets, and on the order form it says, "Sid Bernstein Presents." And that's when I made the connection.

Finally she decided she was going to go with me to protect me. I tried to tell her that she didn't want to be in the middle of that. But I wanted to go so badly, I said fine.

It was probably an hour and a half ride on the subway to get out to Shea from where I lived. We were sitting right on top of one of the dugouts. I remember not being able to hear anything. I remember them coming out through this tunnel and running for the back of the stage, up the stairs and onto the stage. Total bedlam. I don't believe that I actually heard a note of music, and I don't think that's what I was there for. I didn't expect to hear the music, and in those days going to a concert was almost unheard of anyway. When you'd go it would be at a much smaller venue, and I couldn't even picture going there to listen to the music. I just remember them being onstage, I remember their hair moving, and me just kind of losing my mind. At some point, all the other guys were playing their instruments and John just started doing *something*—he wasn't playing.

I had done everything in my power with my partners in crime to get to them. And we never managed to get to them—all I wanted was an autograph. Even just being in the same place with them was enough. I felt blessed to even be there, especially after thinking I wouldn't get any tickets, and then the strange way I got the tickets, and my mom telling me I wasn't going, and me pleading with this woman, like I'll clean up my room for the rest of my life till she finally gave in.

Even at the Ed Sullivan theatre, you're that close to them, you fixate on that one thing, which was McCartney. I know the other guys were there, but I don't remember too much about what they were doing.

Just being in the stadium with all of those people. Who holds a concert in a stadium? I had to be there. I would have gone anyway, with or without a ticket. I would have taken my punishment from my mom or whatever.

* * *

For this Shea Stadium concert, however, things were different from the year before. The Beatles had suffered a few public relations setbacks on the '66 tour, and, after nearly getting assaulted by angry mobs for the unintentional snub of Imelda Marcos, barely escaped with their lives. They had become pariahs in the southern Bible Belt due to the infamous quote from John. Perhaps as a cumulative result, this Shea Stadium concert took place with 11,000 empty seats—something that would have been unthinkable just a year before.

JoAnne McCormack didn't care about the empty seats. Her enthusiasm for the Beatles hadn't wavered in the least. She was just thankful that the concert wasn't cancelled outright—the possibility of which became the topic of rumors leading up to the date.

During the concert, for old times' sake, McCormack squeezed her way into the same field level box right against the railing from which she experienced the '65 event. This time, however, she wasn't content to simply stay in the box.

* * *

JoAnne McCormack: I told my girlfriend I was gonna run onto the field. I knew I'd never make it to the stage, but what the heck, I'd give it the ol' New York try. So I waited till the end, and my pants were so tight, she had to help me lift my leg over the railing. And I said, "Okay, there are three police barricades, I'm going to go under them." I knew they were gonna get me, but I didn't care. It's weird because from the moment I decided to go, I don't have any recollection of what I did. My girlfriend said, "You didn't go under the barricades, you climbed *over* them." I climbed over three police barricades, I have absolutely no recollection of that whatsoever, and she said "There was a cop who was about to run after somebody else, then he saw you, and you ran right to him!" I didn't see the cop, I didn't see the barricade, I didn't see the stage, I didn't hear them playing. The next thing I knew, I felt a tight squeezing around my middle, and I felt my body go limp, and saw my little Keds sneakers being dragged along on the grass, and the next thing I knew I was in the dugout.

So, if you could be passed out *and* moving, I was passed out and moving. So they put us all in the dugout, and after the show was over they ran us down through the tunnels and let us go out the other end.

* * *

The Beatles then flew to the West Coast for the final leg of their final tour. August 25th had them playing the Coliseum in Seattle, followed by a Los Angeles concert in Dodger Stadium on the 28th.

On August 29, 1966, the Beatles played their last concert before a paying crowd, at Candlestick Park in San Francisco.

By the time they had reached San Francisco, they had come to the quiet realization that this would likely be their final concert, period. They were tired, and frustrated with touring and all of its limitations—both creative and logistical. They had seen for themselves the negative as well as positive effects of having virtually all of their words and actions so keenly recorded and reported to the masses. Their continued enthusiasm and unmatched brilliance in the recording studio notwithstanding, the aspects of touring that had begun to wear on them by the end of the '65 tour had positively sapped them of their famous exuberance throughout the '66 tour. It is to the Beatles' great credit, however, that they did not allow their flagging energy to reveal itself while they were performing onstage.

But by the time they had reached Candlestick Park, they knew that the chances of returning to this grind yet again were slim and none.

* * *

Dale Ford: My dad actually drove us to Candlestick Park and my mom came, because she wanted to go. She just loved them, and still does to this day! I remember it to be shorter than the other two concerts. They got out there, they did their thing, they were having a good time because they knew it was their last concert. So I think for that reason, they had a good time. They didn't stay out there long, but they were laughing and joking with each other. They were giddy!

Candlestick Park, how many thousands of people—unbelievable. And when you hear that many people screaming . . .

I don't have the ticket. When my husband and I split up, he got custody of it!

CHAPTER SEVEN

The End of Touring and the Middle Period

The Beatles made no formal announcement, either before or after the Candlestick Park concert, declaring the end of their touring years as a group. They had more reasons to quit touring than they had to continue, and simply carried on with the business of being the Beatles—except from that point on it would be without the prospect of ever playing to stadiums full of screaming teenagers again.

* * *

Betty Taucher: They could not re-create in public what they were doing on records and they couldn't make themselves be heard. The technology hadn't caught up with what they could do. Now I think they would love touring. You could do videos, you could do sounds, you could have walls of speakers and hear every nuance of every song. It wouldn't be a problem, no matter how many people were screaming.

Maggie Welch: I guess if you add it all together, from the very moment John met Paul, they played together for 14 years, not a real long time for a band to survive, but the pressures that they had—imagine traveling all around the world for three years, and never being able to go anywhere. That has to put a strain on your relationship with the other person.

Dale Ford: I was so disappointed when they decided they weren't going to tour any more. Oh, I was heartbroken! And when they got into their more advanced music, when it started becoming deep, really heavy-duty stuff that took a lot of musical skill and talent—when that came about, I liked them and I got every single one of their albums. But I don't think I'll ever enjoy anything as much as the early Beatles. It was so innocent, it wasn't jaded, the music wasn't cynical, it was just fun. It was pure fun. I'll always have a bigger fondness for those early years.

* * *

The Beatles' transition period from their touring-recording regiment to one dedicated solely to studio work met with different reactions from their fans. Some who had missed seeing them in concert lamented having forever lost the opportunity. Others saw it as the end of a special era, and consequently felt their enthusiasm for the group as having reached a peak and then begin to wane. By now, there was a multitude of other British Invasion pop groups following the Beatles to America—The Dave Clark Five, Herman's Hermits, The Hollies, The Kinks, and harder-edged groups like The Rolling Stones and the Who. American teenagers found themselves paying increasing attention to these other groups, thus diluting the concentrated energy that had originally been directed almost exclusively at the Beatles. The difference is that many of the lesser pretenders to the Beatles' throne ultimately proved to be one- and two-hit wonders.

* * *

Barbara Allen: Once that concert in Philadelphia ended, that was the zenith for us. That was the high point of the whole thing. And things started to change, when other groups from England started to get into our consciousness, like the Rolling Stones. And some of the new friends you were meeting liked the Rolling Stones better than the Beatles. Herman's Hermits, the Kinks, the Dave Clark Five—it became this huge soup of rock musicians from England. And while the devotion was to the Beatles, the intensity, at least for me, started to change.

Janet Lessard: Then you get into high school, and you start getting involved in other things, and thinking of other things, so we kind of left it behind. But for those two or three years, it was really something to see.

Debbie Levitt: I know there were a lot of fans back then that did let it go, and never followed it. Or if it wasn't to their liking say, after '65 and couldn't get into *Revolver,* just let it go by.

* * *

Looking strictly at the Beatles' studio output, the period beginning with the release of *Rubber Soul* through *Revolver* is commonly referred to as the Beatles' "middle period," which in turn evolved into their "psychedelic period," which would run through the remainder of 1966 and for the entire year of 1967.

* * *

Cathy McCoy-Morgan: I do love those songs, "You're Gonna Lose That Girl," "The Night Before" and "You've Got to Hide Your Love Away" [from *Help!*]. And they started experimenting a little bit. I enjoyed that evolution of their music. I thought it was really wonderful. And they were so prolific, they just wrote song after song after song. I don't think there was a bad song.

David Rauh: *A Hard Day's Night* was a definite step forward from what they were doing on their two previous albums. *Help!* was kind of a downer because their writing abilities improved faster than their musical abilities. They were writing deeper-thought songs by the time of *Help!*, but their musicianship hadn't improved yet. With *Rubber Soul* and *Revolver* their musicianship really blossomed, and then it went even further.

Maggie Welch: When I heard the song "You Can't Do That," and it was in a minor key, I thought, "Oh! This is interesting. They're already trying something different." Especially with such an excellent producer—a classically trained oboist who could write musical scores for them, because they couldn't read a word of music. A perfect marriage!

Charles Pfeiffer: I kind of enjoyed it when they kind of got off the *A Hard Day's Night* stuff and I really loved the year when they went in and did *Rubber Soul* and *Revolver*. To me, that combination of songs is when they really evolved as musicians and I was like wow, they lead everybody into things, and of course *Sgt. Pepper* and *Abbey Road* are great, but I just love *Revolver* and *Rubber Soul.*

Carol Cox: My favorite Beatles era is the *Hard Day's Night* era. *Rubber Soul* will always be the quintessential album for me. I hated "Eleanor Rigby" at first. I was like, "What's happened to my Beatles? Why are they doing it?" And at that point I was also into other groups like the Monkees, Paul Revere and the Raiders, and some other bands.

I did turn away for a while, but then I turned back. I don't think they ever really left me per se. There's something that always pulls you back.

Wendi Tisland: You know what? I was upset at first. I didn't really care for it. They were changing from the Beatles we knew, their appearances were changing, the music was changing, but I never wrote them off. I still listened. And now that I'm older I know they had to do that, and that's where their best music came from, in their later days.

Janet Lessard: I got as far as *Revolver* with them, then they started getting a little bit funny. And then they got into this mysticism and all this Maharishi business, and that's when we parted ways. I just didn't like that. I liked the simple, early Beatles and to this day I still do.

Barbara Allen: Although I kept up with it a number of years, the music did change a lot, and I started to. Whereas in the beginning we'd play *Meet the Beatles* 24 hours a day, now you would buy the album and you would listen to it a few times, but you weren't obsessing.

And also, *Revolver* and *Sgt. Pepper* took the music to another level. By then they had started to do studio work, they brought in orchestras, that kind of drug-influence thing, I think the music had expanded. It had a whole different sound to it. The early stuff was part and parcel of the early days that were I guess I would say very pure.

* * *

Then there were other Beatles fans who, upon hearing the newer, more varied, and increasingly sophisticated songs emerging from Abbey Road studios, felt an exciting new era just beginning.

* * *

Linda Andriot: The earlier stuff I'm not really into 'cause I guess it's just a little bit before me, because I was young. But when I got into them in '66, we were doing *Rubber Soul* and *Revolver*. I got more into the *Sgt. Pepper* stuff when that came along.

David Rauh: They weren't touring anymore, but what they were doing in the studio was much better than what they had done previously. Every year a new album would come out and be even better than the previous one. I know they lost a lot of fans then, especially the female ga-ga girls who wanted little mop-tops. I know people who said, "As soon as they grew the moustaches I stopped following them." Isn't that odd! I know people who thought the Beatles were great, but didn't follow their solo careers afterwards. How is that possible?

Betty Taucher: I think what amazed us was how much their music grew with them, how much every album was different, how the music got better, more developed. They didn't stay in the same-old, same-old. There were tons of British bands that came out in '64, a lot of whom I liked, but by '66 most of them were gone.

Paul Chasman: They did so many things with harmonies and chord progressions and instrumentation that just had not been done or put together in that way before. And I can still listen to a whole lot of their stuff and go, "My God, that is just *so* clever."

Barbara Boggiano: I liked what they were doing and what they were getting into. I've always been a poet, and their songwriting at the time really influenced my poetry. Their whole way of looking at things really made me think that there was more to this than this rhyming thing. I actually enjoyed their progression. Some stuff, of course, I just never could figure out.

Art Murray: The first time the Beatles whacked me in the head, where I began to really change totally about them, was right at the beginning of my college career, which was '66. Up to that point to me they were still a pop group, they still didn't have any real credibility as serious musicians. I knew *Rubber Soul* and *Revolver* backwards. I had listened to them intently and by the time I was listening to them I was around people who took that music seriously.

Paul Chasman: I got more and more into them as they progressed, because musically they were getting more and more out on the cutting edge. As a musician I progressed along with them. I couldn't care less about the hype and hoopla, in fact it was years before I was able to distinguish which was a Paul McCartney song, which was a John Lennon song, that kind of thing. I was just interested in the music.

Maggie Welch: I knew it was inevitable that they were going to change, and that it would happen fast. When

Revolver happened, and then nothing happened for months, I thought, wow, something's cooking.

* * *

After a prolonged several months in the recording studio, the Beatles released the remarkable "Strawberry Fields Forever"/"Penny Lane" double A-side single in early February of 1967. The two songs were originally planned for inclusion on the upcoming album, but were released earlier to help compensate for the long absence of new Beatles music in the air.

The two songs show both Lennon and McCartney at the height of their songwriting powers, but also further reveal their very individual approaches in recalling their childhood hangouts. Paul's "Penny Lane" is a jaunty stroll through the busy Liverpool neighborhood, full of lyrical imagery and still more experimentation with musical arrangements and new instruments (such as the piccolo trumpet solo) first heard on *Revolver*. John's "Strawberry Fields Forever" offers a more surreal visit to the grounds of the Salvation Army girls' home through which he'd often pass going to and from his childhood home. The final version blends two separate takes, recorded at different tempos, one of which was slowed down creating the rather eerie feel of the piece. The song's atmosphere is also aided by the memorable horn and string arrangement and Ringo's thunderous drumming.

While this single has earned and maintained its status as a true landmark in rock music history, it was still only a precursor to what the Beatles had in store for the world. Word began to spread by the spring that the group was just about ready to unveil their most ambitious work to date, *Sgt. Pepper's Lonely Hearts Club Band*.

* * *

Art Murray: The build up for that release was immense. It was indescribable by today's standards; how it was to be a kid at that age, and know this album was going to be out, and that you probably wouldn't be able to get it for weeks because it would be out of the stores faster than it was in—there would be a line.

But I knew it was coming out, I'm in college, the Beatles are now bona fide, are now established because people I know in college take them seriously. This is real music.

* * *

On June 1st, the Beatles finally released *Sgt. Pepper's Lonely Hearts Club Band*. The album turned the rock music world on its head. The cover itself, featuring the Beatles in brightly colored satin marching band uniforms, standing before a cardboard cutout crowd of celebrities and historic figures, perfectly reflected the burst of musical creativity contained inside. And, for the first time on a rock album, the song lyrics were printed on the back.

The opening sounds of an orchestra tuning up just before the first chords of the title song immediately hinted that this was going to be a very different kind of album. What followed was among the most experimental and imaginative set of songs the group ever created, such as John's surreal wordplay on "Lucy in the Sky with Diamonds," and Paul's heartbreaking "She's Leaving Home" (accompanied only by a string section). As with *Revolver*, every song has its own distinct sound, but this time with an intangible extra ingredient (L.S.D. perhaps?) making each song all the more colorful. The climactic "A Day in the Life" in particular had music observers excitedly talking and writing about its meaning for months after they first heard it. But even without the production techniques, courtesy of the indispensable George Martin, most of the songs themselves, like "A Little Help from My Friends," stood on their own as mini-masterpieces.

Music critics, musicians, and average listeners became mesmerized by the colorful myriad of new musical and sound effects swirling throughout the songs on the album. No less significant was the fact that, for the first time, the song content of American version of a Beatles album had finally coincided exactly with that of the British release. This album was obviously a true and self-contained work of art, not to be rearranged or sliced up and doled out in bits and pieces on future American releases. From this point on, Capitol ceased to tamper with the British releases (although it would still find ways of putting together "new" albums culled from previous releases).

* * *

Art Murray: By the time *Sgt. Pepper* comes out, I can recall—as I recall very few things from that era—I can recall vividly the day I got that album. It was in the window of the music shop, it was impossibly beautiful, because it had almost autumn colors to it, and my recollection at least is that I bought it in autumn, whether I did or not. But I remember seeing that album in the windows and being able to go in and buy it. And it was magical. And at the time, to show you how early this was in my life, my parents had to actually spot me the money. They bought it for me, and I very, very rarely asked my parents to buy me a record of any kind. All my listening was the radio. But I wanted that album. I hadn't heard what was on it yet, really, or had heard some of it, but really didn't know much about it, but it was THE album, and—it's an overused term, but the cultural impact was immense. I went from being a music fan to something a little more than that with the release of *Sgt. Pepper*. Here was this album and all of the things that went with it, and of course at that time you're going from where I was entering college, a kid who was told by his dad if you have to go into the army—there was a draft at that time—make sure you join the ROTC and go in as an officer. Life as an enlisted person is terrible. So I joined ROTC when I went to Fordham.

I was out of ROTC and protesting the Vietnam war within six months. I was wearing shirts with psychedelic patterns on them, allowing my hair to grow, and all the other attendant issues that arose came up at that time.

So it was a wild thing and the Beatles were right at the hub of it. They were, in my experience, leading the parade, in a way that I think today would be unimaginable.

Maggie Welch: And then *Sgt. Pepper* came out and it was clear to me why there was such a break. And it was also clear that they were heavy-duty into drugs! It was just that the change was as radical as it was.

Penny Wagner: With *Sgt. Pepper*, when they started getting into drugs, a lot of people I knew that liked the Beatles didn't like them anymore. I went through the whole thing with them. I thought, maybe they'll straighten out. They didn't look like mop-tops any-more—they had the facial hair, beards. My mother said, "You can't like them anymore, 'cause they're on drugs." I said, "Mom, *I'm* not taking the drugs!"

Claire Krusch: It killed me to hear they were doing drugs. I'm sure every girl who ever fell in love with them—you know you have that little personal rela-tionship with them. You don't want to think they're going to be smoking dope and dropping acid, and smoking cigarettes and getting lung cancer. Not my sweetheart Paul McCartney! But when you're a teenager, that's what your thought process is like. At least for me it was.

Linda Andriot: I loved *Sgt. Pepper*! That was my favorite album of everything. *Sgt. Pepper* is just like, the coolest. All my boyfriends had long hair and would wear the bell bottoms.

David Rauh: By the time we got to *Sgt. Pepper*, everybody was wearing psychedelic outfits and looking for Nehru shirts.

Janet Lessard: I know a lot of music in that period, when they were doing *Sgt. Pepper* and all that stuff, is praised by the critics, but I just didn't like that period. I didn't like their appearance, and I didn't like that music. That was the beginning of the '70s flower child/hippie movement, and I have to say I didn't enjoy them as much.

Betty Taucher: *Sgt. Pepper* was fantastic. That was a big deal when that album came out. Just the cover alone was amazing, when you look at all the imagery that was on that cover. And it had the insert—I still have the Canadian Mountie inside. And you had all the lyrics on the back. That was unheard of!

Harold Montgomery: The very next album was *Sgt. Pepper*, 'cause *Revolver* had already been out when I saw them. I remember going out and buying it and I instantly loved it. The guys seemed to like it, but a lot of the girls that I knew didn't think "Strawberry Fields" and "Penny Lane" were much of anything. By the time *Sgt. Pepper* came out, they said, "Oh, they look so much older now with those moustaches and beards. . . . " But I didn't care about that, so that didn't bother me, and I loved the album. They had crossed over to the Monkees, because the Monkees were kind of the image of the '64 Beatles. I was still buying a lot of the magazines that had Beatles things in them, but they were filling up with Monkees. So I'd tear out the Beatle things, and give the rest of the magazine to the girls who wanted the Monkees.

* * *

The Beatles' psychedelic period reached its peak throughout 1967, but ended rather abruptly after the release of *Magical Mystery Tour* at year's end.

* * *

Cathy McCoy-Morgan: I really loved the *Sgt. Pepper* album in '67. That was phenomenal. They called it the "Summer of Love" and they came out with all their psychedelic stuff. I was wearing the same clothing. I just went the whole gamut with them. However it was, their changes mirrored my life.

JoAnne McCormack: I had a really good bunch of friends. In 1967 I remember my parents had gone away, I was 17, I told them I was going into the city to "a Beatle rally" because the Monkees were at the Warwick and were protesting the Monkees being there because they were just copying the Beatles. And that's where I met a lot of these other people. And we are still friends to this day. Then I went to the Port Authority bus terminal and went to Jersey 'cause I had to stay at my grandmother's house. And that night the *Our World* TV special was on, when they recorded "All You Need Is Love."

* * *

While the Beatlemania era could be considered having ended with the group's final concert tour, their most loyal fans were in no way ready to turn their attentions elsewhere. In August of 1967, a

Beatle fans visit Shea Stadium on the anniversary of their idols' performance there.

One Year Later, It's a Beatle-In at Shea

By Stephanie Roumell

Some 300 teenie boppers staged a "Beatle-In" outside Shea Stadium yesterday. They arrived in busloads in the morning and stayed until late last night.

They talked about the Beatles, they cried, yelled and screamed over the Beatles, but they never laid eyes on a Beatle—nor did they expect to.

The kids came ("Do we have to EXPLAIN to you why we're here?") to commemorate the day last year that the moptop songsters were at Shea to sing and wail.

It was reported that a disc jockey prompted the turnout, but the teenie boppers — mostly girls — were convincingly spontaneous in their Beatlemania.

"We love them! They're our life!" they screamed.

"Give us the Beatles. We want the Beatles," they chanted.

They had a leader and her name was "Johnny." She demonstrated her love for the Liverpool four by suggesting that the youngsters storm Shea Stadium's gates. She was dissuaded when patrolmen said even Beatlemaniacs can get arrested for things like that.

Later, Johnny led a small contingent in when a delivery truck passed through the gates. The police conducted them back out.

After that they remained peacefully in the parking lot in front of Gate B for Beatles.

They offered such gestures of adoration as ripping apart a magazine that featured the Monkees ("They're squaresville") and reciting John Lennon poetry ("It's a groove").

The day was done, the stars came out and the fans filed into the stadium for the Mets-Phillies game. The youngsters never budged from the parking lot.

At 9:15, several fans inside the park heard a long, long screech, the minute that the Beatles made their triumphant entry to Shea the year before and outside on the parking lot not one eye was dry.

Beatles rally at Shea Stadium, August 1967, marking one year since the group's second and final concert there.

group of hundreds of fans gathered outside Shea Stadium in the hours prior to a Mets game to commemorate the one-year anniversary of Beatles' second and last concert there. Their enthusiasm showed no signs of waning.

* * *

JoAnne McCormack: We had several Beatle rallies at Shea Stadium after they had toured. In '67, John and Cynthia were still married and we had the rally on August 23rd, which was the anniversary of the second Shea concert, and it was also John and Cynthia's anniversary. I went to the bakery and got a half-sheet cake with "Happy Anniversary John & Cyn," and we all dove in and had cake, and WCBS radio came and interviewed a couple of us.

Ilona Gabriel: We'd hang around, sing Beatles songs, bring tape recorders and radios, people would bring guitars. We'd go to gate B and stay there all day. There were reporters there and TV cameras. A lot of the news people would be there because such a large crowd had gathered.

JoAnne [McCormack] and I decided we were going to sit on second base the exact moment that the Beatles came onstage. So we climbed a twelve-foot fence and a short wall. We were spotted by guards. We take off, leap over the wall, climb the fence, jumping halfway down, only to be met by a police car. We take off, the car hits a curb and the bumper falls off. We safely made it to the subway.

* * *

On August 25, 1967, Brian Epstein died from an overdose of sleeping pills, ruled accidental by the coroner. The Beatles were in Bangor, Wales, at the time, attending a series of lectures by their new spiritual guru, the Maharishi Mahesh Yogi. Word of Epstein's death shocked the group, who quickly left Wales to return to London.

Even though Epstein's role as manager had been steadily diminishing since the end of the Beatles' final tour, his sudden death left the group feeling direction-less. John cited that moment in later interviews as the beginning of the end of the Beatles, as his desire to move on without them took a firmer hold. Paul, however, was determined to continue creating new projects with his bandmates, and presented the idea of a television special with music (but no real plot to speak of), based on one of his new songs called "Magical Mystery Tour."

On September 11th, a little more than two weeks after Epstein's death, the group began their new film project in a rented tour bus. They had invited a motley group of acquaintances, actors, circus performers, and Beatle employees to take part in the film, which had very little pre-production planning, no script, and consequently no real coherence. Interspersed with brief vignettes filmed at stops in the English countryside were musical interludes, showcasing six new songs, released in the U.K. as a double EP (as with their earlier promo films, each self-contained song sequence could easily serve as an MTV-style music video). The project was filmed in color but aired in black and white on the BBC on Boxing Day (the day after Christmas) in 1967. The reviews were scathing, and the Beatles, for the first time since becoming a worldwide success, had experienced their first creative failure.

The film was never shown on an American television network, but the American *Magical Mystery Tour* LP release included the soundtrack songs plus their hit singles from '67. The album package consisted of a photo booklet of scenes from the film. However, since American fans had not had an opportunity to see the movie, the photos themselves made little sense. But, of course, the songs, such as Paul's "Fool on the Hill" and John's "I Am the Walrus" maintained the high creative standards the world had come to expect from the group.

There had been much speculation as to whether *Magical Mystery Tour* would have even been made if Brian had been alive and had any veto power over the idea. Despite its failure, the Beatles geared up for yet another new phase of their career together.

CHAPTER EIGHT

The Apple Years

n early 1968, the Beatles announced the formation of their own Apple record label. They also bought and converted part of a luxury townhouse at 3 Savile Row in London into a recording studio and Apple offices.

On May 14th, John and Paul flew to New York to promote Apple, give interviews, and appear on *The Tonight Show* (which aired from New York until moving to L.A. in 1972). Host Johnny Carson was not present that night; sportscaster Joe Garagiola filled in.

Once again, savvy New York fans made it a point to track down John and Paul during their brief visit.

* * *

Maryanne Laffin: That was the first time I had actually tried to physically see them outside of a concert. I was 15 at the time. They were staying at the St. Regis Hotel. We were standing in front and they came out of a car and went in, and we were right there and saw John and Paul. And I remember just falling apart and feeling like, "Okay, I can die now!"

Ilona Gabriel: In 1968, John and Paul came to New York to promote Apple. We'd go to the hotels where we knew where they were staying. We'd go to the St. Regis hotel in the morning, and hide out in a linen closet to see if we could catch a glimpse of them in the hallway. We got real dressed up—it was a Sunday morning—and most of the kids chasing after the Beatles were dressed normally, in tight pants, paisley shirts. We didn't do that. We got dressed up, so our hair would be in a ponytail, we'd wear a nice Sunday dress with gloves and a hat and purse. So we just walked right into the elevator. Nobody questioned us, 'cause they just thought we belonged there. We thought we knew what floor they were on and we hid in one of the closets that were open. And you could hear voices in the hallway with English accents, so we knew we were close. But someone did find us before we ever got to see John and Paul. And they did roughly ask us to leave. But we did have a chance to see them because we knew when they were coming out. They'd go to their limousines, so we did see them a few times leaving the hotel. And there was chaos, everyone banging on the limousine windows, climbing on the back, just calling out their names, scrutinizing everything they were wearing. I remember John had on white sneakers and he had a little medallion, the same one he wore when they sang "All You Need Is Love." My mother gave me permission to cut school 'cause it's not usually something I would do. I guess she figured it was better to say yes, rather than me doing it behind her back.

We had the taxicab following them to the airport, 'cause we had the taxicabs lined up around the corner where they couldn't see them. So after we gave them the send off in the limousine, we take off—I'm sure they wondered what was going on because there were probably about twelve of us. Somewhere over the Triboro bridge, the limo did lose us. So we made it to the airport and we knew what airline they were going on, so several of us ended up in different areas. And of course there was no security at that time, so we were running as fast as we could to the gates and to the field. And of course they tried to stop us. We were chased by security guards and airport police. We never did get on the tarmac where the plane was, and never did see them go onto the plane. But it was fun because we went through the motions of it. And we tried!

* * *

On July 17th, the *Yellow Submarine* film premiered in London, with the Beatles (except Ringo) in attendance. The animated film, a fanciful story of the Beatles' adventures in a yellow sub, is a virtual explosion of color and surreal images set to their songs, about as psychedelic as you could get.

The Beatles' involvement in *Yellow Submarine* was in fact quite minimal, and by this point, they personally had already pretty much left the psychedelic era behind. The group was making yet another transition, this time back to a less complicated, more guitar-based rock & roll style.

* * *

JoAnne McCormack: In September of '68, we got all our friends together, 25 or 30 of us, and we chartered a bus and took a sheet and made a big *Magical Mystery Tour* sign like the front of the album. We took the bus up to Bear Mountain and we had three-legged races, a picnic, all this kind of stuff. We wrote invitations inviting people on our Magical Mystery Tour. We called ourselves the "Walrus Cornflake Sitting Society." All kinds of wild stuff.

Maryanne Laffin: The Steinway Piano Corporation had a building on West 57th Street. And one of us, I don't know who—we were all very young, but we rented one of the rehearsal halls there. And we had a Beatles rally there. We made up tickets and fliers. Who would rent this out in a prestigious building to a bunch of kids? It had a piano, and someone in the group played the piano so we played Beatle music and sang, and just had a lot of fun.

Paula Lewis: I graduated high school in 1968. I remember when I was in college, a small local junior college, things were very slow coming in every respect. One day in the student union building, someone had pre-set the jukebox and all day long "Hey Jude" played over and over. And it really bugged a lot of people, but I thought it was just wonderful. And every time I hear it now I remember that day!

* * *

In November of 1968, the Beatles released a new album of songs written mostly during a trip to India to study further with the Maharishi at his retreat. The group wrote dozens of songs, and 30 of them were released on the double album titled simply *The Beatles* (although it was known immediately upon its release, and forever more, as the *White Album*). Its stark, all-white cover marked a 180-degree turn from the bright colors and costumes of *Sgt. Pepper* and *Magical Mystery Tour*.

The 30 songs comprising the *White Album* cover virtually every musical genre of the 20th century. And, although a few were outright throwaways (George Martin wanted to pare it all down to a single LP), the musical range the Beatles cover throughout is nothing short of astounding. There is hard rock ("Birthday," "Helter Skelter," "Back in the U.S.S.R."), a touch of old English Music Hall ("Honey Pie"), country & western ("Don't Pass Me By"), blues ("Yer Blues"), tender ballads ("Julia," "Blackbird"), Reggae ("Ob-La-Di, Ob-La-Da"), and songs that defy strict categorization ("Piggies," "Glass Onion").

It was during the recording of the *White Album* that the Beatles began to fracture. John's growing boredom—and outright obsession with his new love, Yoko Ono—Paul's increasingly bossy way of trying to keep everyone together, and George's frustration over the others' dismissive attitude towards his songs, all resulted in increasing bickering. They began to record a good deal of their songs separately as they never had before.

* * *

Betty Taucher: When the *White Album* came out, at the time I was a senior, and they had sent us on a field trip to Toronto, studying Asian history. The girl I was staying with had the album. She said, "I just got the newest Beatles album," I'm like Oh my God! And she didn't know me, and asked, "Are you a Beatles' fan?" and I said, "Do the Chinese eat rice? Yes, yes!" She brought it out and showed me, and we played it and played it and sat up half the night listening to this album. And I thought when I get home I've got to go to the store.

Maggie Welch: I've never been really crazy about the *White Album*, I have to admit. Although there are some very good songs on it. But generally, I agree with George Martin who said that it should have been a single album, and that would have been wonderful. *Sgt. Pepper* and *Abbey Road* were.

Art Murray: Every album they made since *Sgt. Pepper*, I had the same sense of anticipation—The *White Album*, I sat with a crappy little phonograph with my friends and listened to it cut by cut.

Kathy Albinder: I loved all their albums, in fact we waited for them to come out. We knew they were coming and we would be waiting to buy them. They day they went on sale, we would have it. And I loved their progression. They didn't stay the same, they really evolved. And I love that, because it's like real life. They became different. And they looked so different from year to year. And they were only together a very short amount of time. Things happened so quickly with them . . . and look at how they changed everything.

* * *

Once the sessions for the *White Album* were completed, Paul's concerns about the group's unity led him to prod the others into coming up with ideas for a new project. A somewhat tentative idea for a televised concert in turn led to the idea of filming the group as they wrote and rehearsed the new songs they would perform for the TV special. In January of 1969, the rehearsal sessions for what would eventually become *Let It Be* began, with film cameras rolling. The first two weeks of rehearsals took place in a cavernous sound-stage at the famous Twickenham film studios, but the Beatles, never morning people, could barely drag themselves into the barren, de-pressing set-up for the morning rehearsals. Before the project fell apart completely, the location was moved to their more homey Apple basement studio for the remaining two weeks. Guest musician Billy Preston sat in for "Let It Be" and "Get Back," and the group's lunchtime rooftop concert on January 30th provided a fitting climax to the film, even though the plans for a TV special had been abandoned.

When it came time to pick and choose among the hundreds of hours of audio for the purposes of releasing an album of the sessions, the Beatles wanted nothing to do with it. The tapes were shelved, to be dealt with at a later date.

* * *

Shaun Weiss: Mal [Evans, the Beatles' assistant] was my mentor. And from the time I moved to England, Mal and I became very close. It was more Mal bringing me into their circle. It started out going with Mal to get food for them. Then I started sitting in Abbey Road, which at the time was called EMI Studios. And there used to be a little partition there, and I'd sit there and Mal would tell me to go out and collect books from who wanted autographs, and I would venture back and Mal would sit there, or Derek Taylor, and would sit and sign autographs. If you physically didn't catch a Beatle in front of you and have him sign something, very rarely did they sign anything, especially if it was handed to somebody like me or Mal, or somebody who would sit and sign for them. My door opening came from Mal Evans.

By '69 I was free to come and go because years had transpired and gone by, and I was known at Abbey Road, so when they were doing *Abbey Road* and *Let It Be.* I was around a lot. I sat in on the session for "The Ballad of John & Yoko," which was done at Savile Row in the basement. It was only Paul and John. I sat through the squabbles, and sat through "Here Comes the Sun" that took five days. And I sat through "Across the Universe" and lot of recordings. Unfortunately, I would just sit in a little room. My job was to make sure if Mal needed food for George or whoever was in the studio, I would go with him, because he couldn't drive and carry this stuff back. We'd drive to an Indian place near Marble Arch, and I would just walk in and say "I'm here for Mr. Harrison's food," and we'd go back to the studio and I would sit there.

During the rooftop concert I was off to the side, with Billy Preston, standing against the wall. And it was so cold that day, I was standing with my hood up shivering. I was just freezing. It was being at the right place at the right time, going up there that morning. Just being there and being asked, "Do you want to come up?" What am I going to say, no? It just got so cold on that rooftop. It seemed like a hundred years, but in reality it wasn't very long. Then the police start coming up, and you get shuffled off, and it was almost stopped. You could see they were just freezing. Billy Preston was shivering. It was a great day, a day of being around four men that you idolized. It wasn't something I ever thought would be so important that people would want to hear about it.

* * *

In the meantime, as the original generation of Beatles fans entered college and enjoyed the freedom to travel on their own, it became popular to travel overseas, especially to Europe. Beatles fans, of course, began making personal pilgrimages to London, with the hope of catching sight of a Beatle or two.

* * *

Paula Myers: After their touring, we never lost interest, at least I didn't. We ended up moving to England for a little while. We were hoping to meet Paul. We went to his house in London, and waited outside his house. I think we stayed across the street. Then the postman saw us and said, "Oh, you just missed him, he just left." But this was in 1969, and I think he was with Linda at that time. We missed out anyway on our chance—we were thinking about marrying him.

Shaun Weiss: We were in front of Paul's house, and down on Cavendish Avenue comes a white Rolls Royce. Who gets out but John and Yoko. There were about ten of us standing in front of Paul's house. So all day long girls were pushing the button of the intercom and Paul was answering it. This time John pushed the button, Paul wasn't answering it. So here we are, John and Yoko standing in front of Paul's house, and they're talking to us, saying, "Is Paul in?" So one of the girls said, "Yeah, but we've annoyed him so much that he won't answer the door." So there I am with a little 126 camera in my hand taking photographs, and what does John do? He hops the fence. And I have pictures of him hopping this fence. It's a thrilling thing that it was captured at the time. There are stories that people never know and never hear, and that day, to see Lennon to hop Paul McCartney's fence, was just touching.

Maryanne Laffin: When I was 15, my friend and I spent the summer in London. We went on a tour, the only way our parents would let us go. Once we got there, we sort of ditched the tour and just hung out in front of Paul's house on Cavendish Avenue, and in front of Apple. We bribed Paul's security guard, and got in and took pictures in his backyard. We weren't actually in the house, we walked through the garage into his yard. And then someone was coming in through the front gate, the guard went crazy, and we had to climb over a back fence to get out.

Linda Cooper: I was still buying all their music and right after that is when my friends and I decided we were going to start our England fund. So I graduated from high school in '69, and we went in May of '70. We got work permits through an agency, and that was supposed to be just for the summer, like a three-month work permit. And we thought, well, we'll just go over and check it out. And we ended up staying almost five years! We lived in London. My one girlfriend ended up marrying an Englishman and they live in Maryland now. We had an absolute blast.

And we went to a book signing when Yoko put out that stupid *Grapefruit* book, and John was with her. I told my friends, "I'm skipping work and calling in sick 'cause I'm going!" And I did, and stood in line, and it was awesome to be eye-to-eye with John Lennon even for a matter of seconds was just unbelievable. And that was the book I had signed and I don't know whatever happened to it. Both John and Yoko signed it.

* * *

Recording sessions for what was to become *Abbey Road* began in late April, lasting into the summer. The album was released on September 26th in Britain and October 1st in America.

Many Beatles fans place *Abbey Road* at the top of their lists of favorite or best Beatles albums, even above *Sgt. Pepper* and *Revolver*. It's a subjective thing, of course. But it's hard to argue that *Abbey Road* presented the Beatles at the very height of their powers, showcasing their songwriting, playing, and singing abilities like no other work they had produced before. *Abbey Road* has it all, from "Come Together" to "Her Majesty," and all that falls in between. Hard rockers like "Oh, Darling!" and "I Want You (She's So Heavy)," co-exist with two of George's finest songs ever ("Something" and "Here Comes the Sun"). There is the legendary medley on side two (for those of you who remember LPs), and even a song for the kiddies (Ringo's "Octopus's Garden"). Add George Martin's always brilliant production, and the result is a rock album that comes as close to sheer perfection as any ever recorded.

* * *

> **Paul Chasman:** The *Let It Be* movie was so depressing, like watching an old marriage breaking up. But at the same time, even out of that came some really great songs. To me *Abbey Road* is the absolute pinnacle of their musicianship. It's an incredible way of going out.

* * *

Oddly enough, *Abbey Road* has often been treated as little more than a footnote in many of the best-known historical accounts of the group's music. An exaggeration? Not upon close inspection.

Abbey Road has always suffered from bad timing. If it had been recorded and released as the group's final creative effort, history would clearly acknowledge it as the stunning climax to the Beatles' musical history together. But, as we know, things didn't follow such a neat and simple order.

After the *Let It Be* project was shelved, the Beatles re-gathered their creative energies to record and release *Abbey Road*. Finally, eight months later—on May 8, 1970—*Let It Be* was released in Britain (May 18th in America). This order of events has left the more casual Beatles fans of the world to assume that the melancholy atmosphere of the *Let It Be* sessions revealed the final break-up of the group. In truth, this heavily documented period of the Beatles' worst lethargy, as shown in the film, really lasted only about one month, i.e. January of 1969. Their problems with each other had indeed begun earlier, as their work on the *White Album* got underway, and continued through the recording of *Abbey Road*. But when you look at some of the more highly regarded historical accounts of Beatles history, it is easy to see how Abbey Road has gotten short shrift—due mostly to that unfortunate timing of its release.

The documentary film *The Compleat Beatles* was released in 1982 and was, for many years, the definitive filmed account of their career. Although much is crammed into a two-hour running time, just about every aspect of the group's career and music is covered, with well-written narration read by actor Malcolm McDowell. However, while the *Let it Be* phase of their work is discussed for three and a half minutes, the segment discussing the *Abbey Road* album takes up a mere 1:37—not a lot of attention to an album the narration calls "their most polished production to date." A little later on, the documentary returns to the subject of *Let it Be*, and provides a full-length version of an alternative filmed take of the group performing the title song in the studio. The narration then concludes "The album sounded like what it was destined to become: the Beatles' swan song." This just isn't true, according to the chronology of events.

With the release of the sprawling *Anthology* documentary, we are treated to greater detail and insight into the Beatles' history as the Beatles themselves tell their story. But even here, the segment covering the *Let it Be* sessions takes up a full 30 minutes of running time. A short while later, the entire segment covering *Abbey Road* runs a paltry 7 minutes, and even that includes the uncut version of the "Something" promotional film. George Martin offered on camera that *Abbey Road* was "a very, very happy album, and everybody worked frightfully well." That can be considered rather faint praise for such a major accomplishment, by both the group and by Martin himself.

It can be argued that one reason *Let it Be* is given so much attention in historic accounts of the Beatles is that there is an abundance of both film and tape preserving those sessions, so naturally we would see more of that than anything representing the *Abbey Road* recordings. But this doesn't excuse the almost offhand manner that has so often accompanied mention of *Abbey Road*.

Another example of *Abbey Road* being blatantly overlooked due primarily to the timing of its release came with *Rolling Stone* magazine's special issue of April 21, 2005 issue listing to greatest rock immortals of all time. Not surprisingly, the Beatles took the

#1 spot, but even Elvis Costello's glowing tribute to the group refers to *Let it Be* as "their break-up album," while failing to make any reference to *Abbey Road*.

It was *Abbey Road* that was to be the Beatles' break-up album, and they pretty much knew it at the time they were recording it. *Let It Be* was a creative mess by the group's standards, but putting it in context, that dark period really only took up a month of their lives (although their friction did begin during the recording of the *White Album*). And seeing such a masterpiece as *Abbey Road* get virtually lost in the shuffle of subsequent accounts of the group's career, simply because it was not the last album of theirs to be released, is unfortunate.

CHAPTER NINE

The Break-Up and Solo Years

On April 10, 1970, Paul McCartney announced what had been suspected by the public for some time—although hearing the actual words still came as a shock. The Beatles were breaking up. This was confirmed by the release of the *McCartney* solo album, and a self-interview McCartney wrote up and inserted in the album package, in which he declared that he was leaving the Beatles.

* * *

Maryanne Laffin: I was devastated. It was like losing a parent after your parents get divorced. We had a fear that they wouldn't make music again as individuals. And we didn't want to lose that.

Maggie Welch: I was not surprised by the break-up, I was not surprised that Paul usurped John. It was John who walked up to Paul in the studio and said, "I want a divorce." But it was Paul who blew the whistle because he was making a record and he thought that would be some great pre-publicity. It was just like him. I have a love-hate relationship with Paul, 'cause I'm a vegetarian and I appreciate tremendously the stuff he does for those causes, but he is definitely very good at playing both ends.

Barbara Boggiano: I remember being very, very upset when they broke up. It almost seemed inevitable, but something that was so magical like that . . . unfortunately I got caught up with the fact that Yoko was the "evil woman," and looking back on it now, that was probably unfair. But at the time, it just looked like, how can this be? How can these four people come together and make such fabulous music, and how can they break up like this?

Musically, they needed to branch out on their own. At the time, it was very upsetting.

Valerie Volponi: I thought everything they did was a great improvement over the last. And I know that by 1969 they probably had nothing more in them to do as a group, and I could understand why they wanted to break up. I think they had done everything they could possibly do in music.

Paula Lewis: I grieved mightily when they broke up, just couldn't believe it—hated Yoko 'cause it was her fault!

Dale Ford: I kind of lost John when he and Yoko got together. It didn't seem like they should be together, and who am I to judge! They'd probably still be together today if John hadn't passed away.

David Rauh: My only regret is that they didn't get back together and do at least one show, whether it be at the end of their career—the rooftop concert was a cop-out. They were talking about renting space in Pompeii or doing some kind of ocean liner thing—they could have done anything they wanted to do. Later on, they could have gotten back together and done it. I agree with them when they said by the time they ended touring, they couldn't hear themselves over the screams. Well, if they had toured in the '70s, they could have drowned out the screams, cause all of the other bands were doing that. They never played when they had the opportunity to blow the audience away. The audience was blowing them away.

It was almost like the audience forced them to stopped touring.

Dale Ford: I kept hoping for a Beatles reunion concert. Just one. I don't care where it is, I'll go!

Maybe they were smart not to—leave well enough alone. They quit on top of their game, and better just to leave it like that.

Barbara Boggiano: It was really a tumultuous time, with the Vietnam War, the Beatles were breaking up, and here comes John, really the "troubadour" for peace. I really started paying attention to what he was saying. I really, really liked him, but it was hard to say anything because he had come out with his "more popular than Jesus" comment. Oh, my father just had a fit and a half. "Communist! You're listening to Communist records!" And the war made absolutely no sense. It was a clear-cut case of us, the younger people, versus people over 30, the establishment. There was really a sharp division. My father and I were always at odds at that time. But John and Yoko were very idealistic, and it was probably the way we all felt at the time. A lot of us could relate to what he was saying. That was something that I still carry with me to this day. If something's wrong, I try to right it, and really not be afraid to speak up.

Cathy McCoy-Morgan: I became very politically active, and very active in the Peace movement. So again there was John Lennon and he was "All You Need Is Love" and "Give Peace a Chance" and that whole thing, and again that mirrored what I was doing in my life. It's where my beliefs were, anti-war, so their music evolved as they evolved, as *I* evolved as a human being, as a person.

* * *

On August 1, 1971, George presented a hastily arranged charity concert in New York's Madison Square Garden (actually two concerts—afternoon and evening) for the victims of a typhoon that had ravaged Bangladesh. His friend and teacher, master sitarist Ravi Shankar, had asked George for whatever help he could come up with. George got out his book of phone numbers and soon responded with an all-star line-up that featured the greatest rock musicians of the day: Eric Clapton, Billy Preston, Leon Russell, Bob Dylan, and, of course, the ever-reliable Ringo. With this concert and subsequent release of the film and album, the "quiet Beatle" had become the first post-break-up hero of the group, stepping squarely into the spotlight to play his new crop of songs, plus a few Beatles favorites.

* * *

Ilona Gabriel: George's Bangladesh concert was kind of like a mini-Beatle concert, a little quieter, because you didn't have all of them onstage. I think a lot of people were trying to pretend that they were okay with Ravi Shankar's music. I wasn't one to pretend; it bored me. But as far as greeting George when he came onstage, it was the same as it was for Beatlemania—everyone on their feet, everyone screaming—you could hear your ears start ringing. But once he started to sing, everyone would quiet down and listen to the music. It was a little more subdued, because most of the Beatlemania people were older by that time. And the crowd was older. You had people then who were taking drugs. The six of us never got into any kind of drugs or smoking or drinking.

We really didn't know what he was going to sing, and it didn't really matter. It was just that there he was onstage, and he could have stayed there for two hours and not do anything, and we'd still be happy.

Barbara Boggiano: Mostly I was following Paul. He was out there. But I started to think, "You know something? George is really talented!" He took a bad situation and he actually worked it out quite well for his career. The Concert For Bangladesh was really something for him to go out there and do this. I had never heard of that before. Nobody had gone out and pulled together a concert to help other people. I really started admiring George better.

Linda Cooper: I was privileged enough in '73—I met George out in front of Abbey Road. I'd do anything to meet Paul, and of course never did. We went by his house—that's what we'd do, we'd go to St. John's Wood, we walked by Paul's house on Cavendish Road and thought, "Let's walk by Abbey Road," and George and Mal were coming out, and that was the first time I saw George. It was like "Wow!" He had that really long, long hair. And Mal was protecting him, but he was really sweet and very nice. I have a couple of old pictures that I found that I have of him.

* * *

George toured in 1974, but it was not a very successful tour in the eyes of his fans. He was in a reflective, even somber period at the time, delving ever deeper into his new-found spirituality, as reflected in his early and mid-'70s albums. But George's heavy-handed approach even had some of his close friends turned off by his habit of turning friendly small talk into a sermon.

As always, however, there were fans who found great comfort in George's laid-back manner.

* * *

Dale Ford: I did go to George Harrison's concerts when he broke out on his own. Some of his songs had a nice gentleness to them. They were easy to listen to, and he was into all that Indian music, Ravi Shankar . . . And that was a kind of peaceful—I wasn't a flower child, I never got into the hippie stuff, even though I lived in San Francisco, I never went that route. But for some reason, I just liked George Harrison. He was very likeable, his music was very soft, very soothing, and easy to listen to.

Jim Rugino: I saw George's tour, at the Cow Palace. It was so late in the tour, he had no voice. And he's singing, and I'm like, what is he doing? And it gets to the chorus, and it's "In My Life."

* * *

Paul was riding high with Wings at this time. The first "official" Wings album, *Red Rose Speedway*, was released in May of 1973. The tour was extensive and, not surprisingly, tremendously successful.

* * *

Penny Wagner: I saw Paul at the Milwaukee Brewers stadium. He came with Linda, who I will absolutely always treasure. I had front row seats. It was totally different from the Beatles concert. At that concert, I was 12 years old, and I still fit in with all the crazy kids. When I went to the first concert that Paul had with Wings, I was yelling, "Baby, you can drive my car!" because that was my favorite song, and he looked down at me and nodded, and that was the first song they played. I almost cried. And nobody around me knew the words, and I didn't even catch myself until the fifth or sixth song, until I looked around and all the people were staring at me. These younger kids were wondering how the hell I knew the words to all these songs. One guy next to me said, "How do you know . . . ?" I said, "Well, you're 25 or 26 years old? I'm 47. I grew up with them! They're a part of my life!"

JoAnne McCormack: I've seen it at a lot of Paul's concerts: You've got the 20-year-olds up in the first couple of rows, which annoys the heck out of me to begin with, because they haven't a clue, they've missed the whole Beatlemania thing. And they're watching and enjoying the concert, and then you've got the rest of us in the back, people from the '60s who really lived through the whole thing, and we're hysterical!

Paula Lewis: When they first came out, I loved Paul. He was the cute one, he had the cute voice, and so on. Then when they broke up, I got much more into George, because he seemed to be more in tune with my life at the time. I didn't really become a big fan of Wings—I still like Paul's music, but I didn't follow him like before. George seemed to take his music in a different direction that I was more in tune with. And it surprised me because he was so quiet.

* * *

On the evening of December 8, 1980, as John and Yoko were returning to their home at the Dakota in Manhattan after a recording session, John was fatally shot by deranged "fan" Mark David Chapman. John's death sent shock waves around the world, leaving his fans virtually inconsolable.

* * *

Debbie Levitt: I met John the day he died. It was a wonderful experience. He and Yoko would go to a coffee shop on Columbus Avenue. And they were frequent there, it was common knowledge but being New York, everybody left them alone to do their own thing

They were coming out, I was walking across, and it was like fate. We stepped out of the door, and I had passed them, and something said "Turn around," like if you get hit, like "bing!" And he turned around and I turned around, we pointed and—he doesn't know me from whatever—and we waved. We walked a few feet, turned around, and he was still looking. So we walked together and met up again and I said, "Good morning, how are you, we're so happy the album [*Double Fantasy*] is out, we're looking forward to the tour . . . " And I turned away. We walked away, came back again and we finished the conversation, and I said, "I really really hate to do this because you're really a private person. Could you please sign something?" So I pull out a piece of paper. They signed, "John Lennon" and "Yoko Ono Lennon." And it was just amazing. We said goodbye and walked away, and the one night I don't watch the news, my friend calls

me and says, "Did you hear what happened to John?"
I said, "No, what happened?" She said, "He was shot."
And because she has such a weird sense of humor, I
said, "Okay, I'm going back to bed." And she said,
"No, no, no!" "And I said to her, "Was he killed?" and
she said "Of course he was killed!" And I've met policemen that patrolled that watch. They told me that
they had to retire, had to give up the force because
of the devastation and the trauma was so bad for
them, that they couldn't help him. They just couldn't
stay a police officer anymore.

Claire Krusch: I was absolutely devastated when he
was killed. It was almost surreal. I just couldn't believe
it. But that's when you realize they're human beings,
that bad stuff happens.

Paula Myers: John was always interesting to me, but he
never really grabbed me. But maybe it was this Yoko
Ono thing. I really didn't like her. I remember when
he was killed—it was very sobering and very upsetting.

* * *

John's murder sent Maggie Welch into an emotional tailspin, but
after a slow recovery, she traveled to England in 1983 as part of a
chartered Beatles tour. It proved a therapeutic trip.

* * *

Maggie Welch: The word got out, not from me, but
somebody told that I had actually seen the Beatles in
person. And a whole bunch of kids, about 18, 19, 20
years old, came up to me and said, "Did you see the

Beatles in person?" And I said, "I sure did. It was Wednesday, the 26th of August, 1964. They came on-stage at ten o'clock, and they left at 10:33." They said, "Will you tell us the story?" And I said, "I'd love to tell you the story." So we sat down in this wonderful lobby of the hotel, near the fireplace, and they all just sort of gathered around me, and I gave them every single detail of the day. You could hear a pin drop. It didn't seem to bore anybody at all, and I went through the whole thing. I felt like an old sage pass-ing the wisdom of the ages to the next generation.

Betty Taucher: I went to see Paul when he came here in 1990 and played at the stadium, soon before they tore it all down and built the new one. And his limo came right by me and the window was open and I saw him close up, like if the Second Coming had hap-pened . . . then he went in to do his practice set. They put the gate down part way, but if you got down on your knees, you could see him. So we were thinking "Only for Paul!" Only for a Beatle would you get down on your knees on the ground and look through the gate to see somebody.

Dale Ford: I've been to all the Paul McCartney con-certs. He has one coming up in Des Moines, and he's never played there before. I can't wait. I love it. He plays all the Beatles' stuff! He just keeps going like the Energizer Bunny. And he puts on a good two and a half to three hours of music. You pay a lot of money, but you get a lot of music.

* * *

On December 1, 1991, after a long absence from the stage, George began a 6-venue, 12-concert tour of Japan, performing with friend Eric Clapton and his band. Clapton had suggested that George get back onstage again, but it took some convincing. It would be George's first tour of any kind since 1974, and his first in Japan since 1966. Clapton had already been touring for his album *The Journeyman*, and, by using his own band and lighting and sound crew, made this experience as easy and comfortable as possible for the anxious George. During the concerts themselves, Clapton remained a sideman, and, except for playing a mini-set of his own hits, let George have the spotlight for each performance.

* * *

Debbie Levitt: I cashed in an insurance policy to see Harrison and Clapton in Japan for six concerts. I saw all six shows. I said, "Look, if you're not coming to me, I'm coming to you." And I don't regret that. The most incredible thing. People were literally weeping, and then for the last show, he brought his son onstage. He looked incredible, just to see him up there and do it. Like McCartney, he could sit up there and read the phone book, it doesn't matter! He had no plans to go out on a tour. He just did it for the fun of it. I'm so glad I went because that was the last concert he did.

Claire Krusch: Growing up as a 13-year-old, I kind of looked up to these guys as superheroes, and nothing bad was ever going to happen to them, and they're kind of immune to the pain that we all feel. And of course as you get older, you realize that we all have our stuff. And when Paul lost his wife, just listening to him talk about the intense grief that he felt, and of course when George died—these guys had a turbulent relationship at times, and this is stuff that we all didn't see and hear about. We thought they were immune to that. They were the Beatles. Never would they have real feelings. But they too experience loss and grief, and hurt and pain, just like anybody else. Just because they're famous doesn't mean that they don't have the same struggles that we have.

I heard Ringo talking about when George was dying of lung cancer, and that's what my dad died of, how he took his hand, and it was just so sweet, such a sweet interview.

Wendi Tisland: When I went to Liverpool in 2001, it was just about the same time that Paul was doing a poetry reading in London. A friend of mine had been there the week before and saw a small clipping about it, otherwise I wouldn't have even known about it. So I went up to Liverpool and did the whole tour, went to Paul McCartney's house and was thrilled with that. They had headphones for the tour through the house, and he was on it, and so was his brother Mike. I was alone in the house, and I went up and sat on his bed where he wrote music—it was very moving. Then I explored the city, went to the Cavern, had a drink, bought a couple of T-shirts, and just got a feeling of the times, even though it wasn't the original Cavern. I had a wonderful time.

When I went back to London, I went to the poetry reading. It was very nice, Paul did some poetry of his own, and he did a couple of songs, and at the end of the event, some of us went to the alley by the stage door to wait for him to come out. It was raining and I didn't have my umbrella, but we stood out there for a good half hour. And then he came out, and I was saying to myself, "Say something!" Then I thought, "No, don't be a jerk, don't say anything." "Say something! You'll never get the chance again!" So he was just getting into his car, and I said, "Hi Paul!" And he gets up out of his car and looks at me and says hello. It was like I was 17 again. My heart was going pitter-pat and I couldn't think of a word to say, 'cause he looked at me like, "Are you gonna say something?" And I didn't.

* * *

In 2003, Ringo's All-Starrs tour included a gig in Milwaukee. Penny Wagner was working as a part-time chauffeur one particular evening when she found herself picking up Ringo and the band at the airport for an unforgettable drive.

* * *

Penny Wagner: Ringo is the neatest human being in my life. I dated someone in another limo company in Milwaukee, who drove Paul McCartney the year before. And Paul had bodyguards. He couldn't open the door for Paul, he couldn't do anything but sit in the car and drive. I got to meet Ringo, up close and personal. He came out of a private jet hangar, called Signature, in Milwaukee. He didn't even want limousines—that's how down-to-earth he is. He asked for this plain black van. For twelve minutes I got to drive him to the hotel. I never met anyone with that high a stature in my limousine driving years that is that down-to-earth. And he had his All-Starr band with him. He had Sheila E., he had Bono . . .

My limo company just told us we had a pick-up at Signature. They didn't tell me that we were picking up Ringo Starr. When I saw Ringo, I couldn't even speak, because I didn't think he was going to get in my van. There were two vans there, and they ushered him in and he said, "I'm getting in the front seat."

I could hardly breathe. And I got to tell him, "You've probably heard this from hundreds of thousands of people—I'm not a fanatic, I just want to let you know one thing. Since I've been twelve years old, I've never ever had a favorite singer as much as you." I said, "I think you're fantastic, I always will, you're a down-to-earth person, and animal lover. . . . You've always been my favorite Beatle, and you always will be." He dressed in black jeans, a New York Yankee jacket and baseball cap, black-and-white high-tops, black sunglasses—it was nine o'clock at night—he was incredible. And he was shorter than I thought he was. He was little. I could hardly even look at the road. I just had to get them there safely.

He asked if we could go to the side entrance of the hotel instead of the front, because he was going to go sign autographs later. He was real concerned about the fans, which was really incredible. He is just a wonderful person. I didn't ask him to sign anything because his privacy is everything . . . unless they offer, I don't do it. And the guy I was dating surprised me and bought tickets to the concert. So I got to go to the concert the following night. So that's why I couldn't drive him the following night!

CHAPTER TEN

The Original Fans Today

Debbie Levitt: Everyone tells me, "Why don't you grow up?" I don't live in the past, I live in the present, but my past is so much part of my daily life. I'm so Beatle-attached that I can't detach myself. When Paul was here (on tour) three years ago, I saw him 49 out of 50 times. The four of us that travel—we get in a van. Forget the car, forget the kids, forget the husband, we're going. And we just make the circuit. And Paul knows me by face, by name. Ringo does also. But I tell my husband, "You're lucky it's every other year that they play—when he comes and we know the schedule, bye-bye, I'm gone. It's not a question of I love you more or less, but"—not that he suffers because he goes to the concert with me. I took my mother, and she met Paul and Ringo. But he understands that it's not so much a passion, but it's a way of life. I do think of other things and I do have another life, I get on with it, but when we get the tickets and things like that, everything stops.

I saw everything in the solo years—The One-to-One Concert, the Bangladesh concert, all of the Wings concerts, Ringo's All-Starrs, every single thing. I've seen them in Spain, Paris, Mexico, all over this country, in Canada. It's the only thing that I live for. I can tell you the catalogue number, the b-side, when it was released, that's the way I have my Beatle collection in my head.

Betty Taucher and daughter Julie in their Sgt. Pepper uniforms at a Chicago Beatlefest.

Betty Taucher: I have a Sgt. Pepper costume that I wear for

Beatlefest in Chicago. A lady from my church made it for me. She's into costuming and she made me an exact copy of Paul's Sgt. Pepper suit. So I wear that when I go to Chicago.

Dale Ford: I was in California taking care of my mother who had hip replacement surgery. And while I was cleaning out her bedroom closet I found an old purse of hers and inside was a Beatles ticket in mint condition for their last concert, at Candlestick Park.

I almost fainted. My mom was doing her rehab exercises on her bed at the time and she thought maybe I had found a dead mouse in that purse or something when I screamed out loud. I came down from the step stool and showed her, and she was really happy for me, but I scared her to death, poor woman! I was so elated I could

Dale Ford and a long-lost ticket for the Beatles' final Candlestick Park concert in '66.

hardly stand it. Mom had gone with me to that final concert. I had long since lost my ticket, but she hadn't. What a mom!

I am still in disbelief that I discovered it after 40 years! The ironic part is that I found it the same week as the 40-year anniversary of their final concert.

Maggie Welch: I only have one really hard and fast Beatle buddy now, and we go out on every Beatle birthday and have lunch together, as one of our traditions. We always set aside time for them after all these years.

Debbie Levitt: Every February 7th, as a tribute, I take the same pilgrimage—my husband cannot understand this—I go back to my old building, and start the trek again: I go to the airport, I look up and watch, then I take the same trek back to the Plaza, and I do the same thing as my memorial, my tribute to them, every February 7th. It's just my thank-you to them for coming here.

Betty Taucher: The eighth grade English class in my school was doing a poetry section and the English teacher said, "You'll never guess what's in the book—the Beatles." The day before I brought in all my Beatles stuff and put it all over her room. . . . I can remember her being so excited by "When I'm Sixty-Four" because she said, "You notice it never mentions love, more like a contractual marriage. Nowhere does it say anything about love."

David Rauh: I have a huge collection of their records from all over the world. Around 1970, I remember the first imports I saw were in a bookstore in downtown Cincinnati. They had a number of Beatle records from England. And I was looking at them and thought, wait a minute, this has a different cover! And I flip it over, and the track listing is different! So I bought a couple of them, took them home, and they sounded better than the American copies. So I went back and gobbled up as many as I could. It's been an obsession ever since. Just recently I picked up one of their singles from Lebanon—"Let It Be/You Know

My Name." The vinyl is in near-mint condition and has the center plug in the middle of the hole. I bought it from a guy in Beirut. And I wrote him an e-mail and asked how many Beatle records are pressed in Lebanon? He said they only pressed vinyl records in Lebanon for about nine years.

Linda Cooper: My son could sing "Help!" before he knew a nursery rhyme. He still likes that song. The other day he went down and got a bunch of boxes and pulled out some songs and says, "You gotta hear this, mom!" and puts on "While My Guitar Gently Weeps" and I said, "Well, yeah!" You know? It's so wild to see the reaction sometimes.

Deborah McDermott: To this day, I'm very proud of the fact that my daughter considers the Beatles her favorite group. To this day, I listen to their stuff all the time. I've never stopped listening to the Beatles. You can go back to them over and over again. And it's not just reminiscing. The more sophisticated a listener you are, the more sophisticated you are with music, you can pick up all this fabulous stuff in them. You can't as a kid.

Paula Lewis: I've been telling my family that for Christmas this year, I want the Beatles CDs. I bought all of the albums when they came out, and I do still have the damaged album covers, with the albums in them, but of course you can't play them. And I bought all of the Beatles' 8-track tapes for the car, and of course those have gone the way, and so over the years I have bought all of the albums on CD. I have three sons, and all of the albums are gone. This one blames that one, and this one blames the other one, but it still is a fact that I don't have those albums any more. So I've just started telling people I want those Beatles albums for Christmas.

Leslie Barratt: As I was looking at their albums again when my daughter got interested, and I started listening to them with her when she was 12 or 13 years old—and when my son was 12 or 13 he got interested in them as well. Some of this may be because when I was pregnant with my kids, I played classical music, Pete Seeger, and the Beatles, and not a lot of other stuff! They've both really gotten into the Beatles as they became teenagers. In listening to them more recently, I realized the thing I really liked about the Beatles' songwriting as it got more sophisticated, was the poetry of it. I particularly liked Paul's lyricism. John was brilliant and kind of political, but the songs he wrote by himself don't have the interesting wordplay that Paul's have. I'm a linguist, so to me, Paul's songs are really interesting. But the two together just got better and better.

Betty Taucher: I had my 8th grade do "In My Life" for their essay. I gave them a copy of the lyrics and played them the song and said, "I want you to go home and tell me what you think the writer is saying in that song, what is he writing about, what does it mean to you." And I brought in albums to show them what it looks like, and 45s and the little things that you stuck in the 45s, and said, "You had to stick this inside the 45 to make it play, because all I had was a record player."

"Where's your stereo?"

"What stereo? None of us had a stereo, we had record players. You'd carry it around with you, 'cause could take it from somebody's house, to somebody else's house when you had a sleep-over or whatever. And you'd play one record at a time."

Shaun Weiss: To this day, if you walk around my house, it's like a shrine to the Beatles. My 40 years as a fan, and then becoming a friend, was a great thrill to me.

Carolyn Long Paulk: One whole wall in my house is devoted to Lennon. He was always ahead of his time. He was so adamant about peace and love, how to get peace, away with the war. And if people could just listen to that, it would be so much better. And of course Vietnam was going on at the same time, and I just thought he was way ahead of his time. Even today his words mean so much.

Janet Lessard: To this day, I enjoy Paul McCartney very much. Out of the four of them, he's the one that kept closer to that original music—uplifting, a nice beat, happy music, nothing really heavy. Of the four of them, once they went their separate ways, he's the one who kept that kind of music going.

Janet Lessard today.

JoAnne McCormack: We e-mail each other [about Paul's concert tour] and we say "I can't believe we're still doing this after 40 years!"

* * *

JoAnne finally met Paul a few times in the early '90s by standing and waiting outside hotel entrances, catching his eye and daring to give his jacket sleeve a yank as he passed by.

* * *

Maryanne Laffin: After Paul's concert in Miami, we drove all night and arrived in Tampa at seven in the morning. Then we got to see him at the Tampa concert. I called a broker to get me good tickets for the Madison Square Garden concerts.

Wendi Tisland: When Paul toured in 2002, I flew down to Dallas to see him, because he wasn't coming here [to Minneapolis]. Then it turned out about two months later he came to Minneapolis/St. Paul, so I saw him again. And a year ago. So I'm still on the Beatle bandwagon! And I converted my niece. When my father died, the funeral was 28 miles away, and I had my nieces in the car, and I continually played *Let It Be* on the way. And they were like, "What a cool song!" So she went to the library and took out the Beatles CDs, and now she's a fan. It just goes on and on.

CHAPTER ELEVEN

Reflecting

The original fans who first heard the Beatles in the late days of 1963 and early days of '64 had no idea at the time (although some have claimed otherwise) that over 40 years later they would still be listening to the Beatles, talking about them, and feeling a genuine sense of appreciation for having experienced them as teenagers. The Beatles, unlike so many of their contemporaries and musical descendants, were not merely a passing phase. The sheer creative quality of their music, plus any number of intangible personal qualities they possessed, enabled them to rise above all other rock groups before and since. And on these closing pages the very same devoted teenage fans, with the benefit of their life experiences and maturity to shape it all into perspective, express what the Beatles still mean to them as that special era continues to recede into history.

* * *

Debbie Levitt: I don't regret any second of it whatsoever. I have my memories, I have my memorabilia, my hopes and my dreams were fulfilled. I'm one of the lucky ones to have met them, and I wouldn't have traded any second of it, and I would re-live it all again. It was all in the timing for me. I always told my mother "Thank God I was born at the right time."

Maggie Welch: I was 13 years old for most of 1964 and just the right age to feel the extreme excitement, joy, charisma, love, anticipation, passion, charm, and music that the Beatles brought to me and thousands of others, which I believe will never be superseded by an other band, ever.

JoAnne McCormack: I'm probably one of the very few people that would love to go back to my teenage

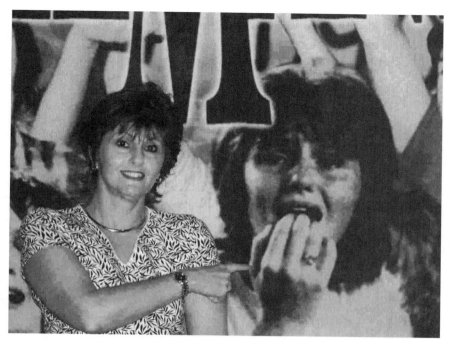

JoAnne McCormack is beside herself at the Madame Tussauds museum in New York. She is standing alongside a blowup photo of her in the stands at the '65 Shea concert.

years and it's basically all because of the Beatles. It was such a good time. Beatlemania was probably one of the best things in my life.

Janet Lessard: More so than the Beatles, who I really did love, I have a soft spot in my heart for that time. It was really a very innocent period. Nowadays the kids grow up much quicker, they're exposed to a lot of different kinds of music, the lyrics are much different—television programs, movies for that matter— the kids are exposed to this at a very early age. And we were not exposed to that. And it wasn't that I just lived in a very closed community. We were quite up to date on things. But there was an innocence about that time. Just the fact that going to the concert—my mother was very protective but she didn't worry about the concert. My father waited around the corner, of course, in the car, but there was no fear or anything of what could happen at a concert at that point. It was just a more innocent and safer time. The Beatles awakened all of these strange feelings we all had: our favorite Beatle, we all kind of fantasized a little bit about that one, we agonized when each one would get married, one by one, but it was much simpler in those days.

Art Murray: For me at least, and for a lot of kids thoroughly middle class—not upper, either, just middle class, white—the Beatles represented the true vanguard. What they did was more than just a musical statement. It had a lot to do with how you visualized how you were going to look, what you were going to do, what you're gonna think. For me, and for a lot of people like me, the Beatles represented models of a sort. I never was naïve enough to think I wanted to be exactly like them, but nonetheless, they were cool.

What they did was interesting, it seemed to have integrity. Their insistence on making music that they wanted to make, on changing the music they made, on developing it and refining it, on making music that was challenging, on attacking issues in their music that frankly they didn't have to attack. And I guess it did have adverse commercial consequences— politics, the Vietnam war eventually—all of that was extremely appealing. It simply corresponded with what kids like me were ready to absorb and internalize. They had a lot to do with how I approached politics—more in the sense that they validated a lot of things. The reason I protested the Vietnam war is because I thought the war made no sense. The Beatles certainly didn't have anything to do with the war or organizing protests. But, by associating themselves with us, by turning what was frankly a political matter that had specific personal consequences at that time for kids like me, cause I could get drafted . . . as much as they were leading, they were also identifying.

Barbara Boggiano: I had a boyfriend in high school, he was a couple of years ahead of me, and he died in Vietnam in '66. And that's what really brought it all very much home to me. For the longest time it was hard for me to even talk about it. But it was all part of the same thing. And the Beatles were right in there with us, promoting the same things that we all felt.

Jim Rugino: When they came out, we were young kids, and they were like teenybopper idols. As we were growing up through adolescence, and maturing through high school, they were too. With the cover for *Rubber Soul*, we saw, for the first time, the Beatles as the adults they were going to become. Their transition from boys in a band to adults in the outside world was at the same time we were making our own transitions. They left the comfort of their "home" the same week we left the comfort of our own homes. The timing was phenomenal. There's meaning there that I haven't yet figured out. It went from pure fun, to drug experimentation, to the serious stuff about the war.

Deborah McDermott: The innocence changed markedly by the time I was about 16 years old. Kids were smoking pot and sniffing glue, it was a very different time. When I was a junior or senior in high school, I had really lost touch with the more psychedelic stuff. I didn't understand it, it didn't ring true to me. I lost a lot of contact with them—not to say all of it, because some of it I thought was fabulous. But some of it, I just didn't get it. Now I do.

Maryanne Laffin: They were such an important part of my life, every single part of my life. And I'm so happy I had the chance to be involved with it and get these friends that I still have today from my Beatle days. I felt like I grew with them as they grew—as they started going into the psychedelic period and the drug period, we were right along with them.

Betty Taucher: It wasn't just the music. It affected everything. And I don't think anybody's done that since, and I don't think anybody will. It just fit the time. I think because the world itself was so violent—you had the war, and we had riots at that time—other riots in other cities, Kennedy's death, and so I think the music was your envelopment and your escape. Here was this beautiful fun music and these gorgeous guys to look at, each of them very talented, in their own right.

Mary Ann Collins: I don't know that we had an appreciation for how historic it was in terms of our involvement. I thought of myself as lucky to be able to go to the concert, but I didn't think of how fortunate I was to have happened to be born at this particular time, and that just as I was in my heyday as a teenager, the Beatles were in their prime. But now I look back and I really feel so fortunate, and so blessed, because at that age, you're so sensitive to everything, and everything is so magnified a thousand times in terms of its importance. In those junior and senior years of high school, the Beatles were just everything. It was just so exciting and so cool, so much fun.

Charles Pfeiffer: I still look back when a Beatles song comes on the radio or if I throw in a CD or something, I could still feel what I felt when I was 13 or 14 years old. I can even see myself sitting in

Charles Pfeiffer today.

front of the television—I've got the DVD of *The Ed Sullivan Show* and I'll throw it in once in a while, and the memories flood back. And everybody kids me— my wife, my kids, everybody who knows me knows I'm kind of a Beatle nut. Not as much anymore, but it led me into playing the guitar, and we formed a band, and played a local circuit, and did a little recording, up through the '70s.

When George died it was really hard. You don't realize how much you miss those guys that are gone, too, that they'll never be together again.

Barbara Allen: This is always happy stuff because everything has changed so much for all of us over the years. It represents I think a time that was so wonderful, innocent, pure that way—so different from how we're all living today. It was a holdover from generations back because it seemed like even though this was a big thing, it was in the context of an ordered world. We all lived with our two parents, and we had family, and neighborhoods, and it was ordered.

Suzanne Milstead and Barbara Allen, still pals and Beatles fans today (see photo on p.144).

Betty Taucher: Apart from the music, when I think about it, each of them meant different things. John inspired me to write, and George was my spirit, Ringo made you laugh at yourself and not take yourself too seriously, and Paul was my romantic fantasy. Everybody has one, he's mine. My girlfriends and I talked a while ago, which Beatle would you like to be with. And we talked about what we thought it would be like, and how we thought each of them impacted us. Because everybody I know is still a fan. I'm a major one still, I'm Beatle-crazy, but most people I know still like them and still listen to their music, even after all these years, they would still say one of their favorite bands is the Beatles.

Those were the best times, all through the '60s like that. It's part of growing up. I think they helped with growing up, they are a part of your identity, their music was a lot of your feelings, and I think the things they did with their music, how much variety, the things that they could do and the sounds they could make. When you listen to music now and realize that most of it is because of what they did.

Maggie Welch: Their unbridled enthusiasm—they didn't get up there and just run through their tunes. John gave you his soul and Paul gave you his heart every single time they sang a song. It's very, very powerful and did change my life.

Paul Chasman: And I have to say on a bigger scale than that—what I think maybe was the most significant to me about the Beatles was how much they grew and how much they always challenged the boundaries, and never seemed to be satisfied with where they were. They were always trying to grow and do something interesting, and creative and exciting. To me, that was one of the most important models I had for how I wanted to live my life. And so I'd have to say that, more than anything as I look back on it, was the most significant influence they had on me.

Maggie Welch: We have so many transplanted people in Colorado now, when I tell people I saw the Beatles at Red Rocks, they go "Whoa! You saw the Beatles at Red Rocks?" And I say, "I sure did—on Wednesday, the 26th of August, 1964!"

I think that the only negative impact that it had on me is that I put my violin down, and never picked it up again. But it's a good trade-off, because I got so much from them—not just from their music, but from their ideas, and from the work that they did in the world, that Ringo and Paul are still doing, trying to make things a little bit better before they take their final bow. I can't imagine what my life would have been like without them, especially as a teenager. I feel that they literally saved my life. If I hadn't had their music and their foresight to tap into from time to time, I don't know what I would have done.

Barbara Allen: And each one kind of represented— I think of Ringo, will always be the Beatle I favored, cause he takes me back to those early years. Lennon I admired for the activism that he got involved with, his commitment to the peace movement. I thought his relationship with Yoko was really interesting, how he became a househusband and she went to work. Paul and Linda I loved because I'm a person who has a devotion to animals. So all their work for animal protection and animal rights I thought was really extraordinary. And George explored the spiritual realm. He was a very spiritual person, and I admired that in him. All of them were so unique and very special human beings, just amazing. And, on another level, the women in their lives really changed how we looked at ourselves. That was a big influence in the '60s.

Claire Krusch: When you get older you just kind of appreciate it a little bit more, too. And you think, "Okay, where was I when I heard this the first time?" that sort of thing. It gives me an appreciation of— take, for instance, my parents, and when they would hear a Frank Sinatra tune. And I kind of smile now because I understand when they'd hear it and they'd start singing and they'd smile, and they'd start, "I remember when . . . " This is what happens now when I hear a Beatles song! My kids roll their eyes. It's something that comes full circle. And you hear it, and sometimes I get a big lump in my throat, for what has been and where they have gone.

Deborah McDermott: They were really miraculous. They were of a time, and of an age, that you can't repeat today. They were an amazing influence on people. I have this memory of being 13 or 14 years old and just—almost swooning—of being carried away. But it was a package deal. It wasn't just the music, it was the package deal of the icon of the Beatles, of the elusive boyfriend of the Beatles, that all came together for just a few years. And when I think that I was part of that, and I think there was a really different thing to be a female at that time, and to experience that kind of euphoria.

Maggie Welch: I came full circle when I became a DJ for KDOD, the classical station in town, in 1977. And I worked there for 12 years, and the whole time I was there I kept saying to everybody, "Mark my words, the Beatles will be the classical music of our time." And they just sort of giggled and pat me on the head, you know. But I think I've been proved right.

Shaun Weiss: In my life, besides my children being born, and the person I love dearly, the Beatles influenced me beyond control. I knew people who fell in love with drugs. My obsession wasn't alcohol, or smoking, or doing drugs. My drug became the Beatles.

Valerie Volponi: If the Beatles weren't out, I have no idea what I might have been interested in. I look back on that and I think I could have gotten into a lot of trouble in that age group, but I didn't. I think it was because I was grounded in the Beatles.

Ilona Gabriel: They never went out of my mind at all. Even now, if things are overwhelming me, thinking about the bills and the house, I'll go and put on my Beatle music. And it just relaxes me, it brings me back to that time when everything was happy. It's excellent therapy. It takes you back.

Carol Cox: I'm glad that I lived through the time, because you had to be there to understand that the Beatles influenced every single thing that was going on at that point, especially if you were young. They influenced our way of thinking, the clothing they were wearing, guys grew their hair—you couldn't live through that era without being influenced by the Beatles. And whether you realized it or not, you *were* influenced by the Beatles. I feel very blessed. The Beatles are a part of me, and that's something that will always be.

JoAnne McCormack: That was my life. My entire life from the time I was 13 until 19 or 20. I was at the right place at the right time. I met my husband when I was 18, we got married when I was 20, and I said, "I love you but I'm gonna tell you right now, there will always be a little piece of my heart for the Beatles." We were just absolutely crazed.

Bibliography

The following books were most valuable in helping me do my job of maintaining the historical context, continuity, and filling in the gaps between contributions by the interviewees.

Badman, Keith. *The Beatles: After The Break-Up*. London: Omnibus Press, 1999.

Lewisohn, Mark. *The Complete Beatles Chronicle*. London: Hamlyn, 2003.

Schaffner, Nicholas. *The Beatles Forever*. New York: McGraw-Hill, 1977.

Spitz, Bob. *The Beatles: The Biography*. New York: Little, Brown & Company, 2005.

Spizer, Bruce. *The Beatles Are Coming!: The Birth of Beatlemania in America*. New Orleans: 498 Productions, 2003.

Books Available from Santa Monica Press

www.santamonicapress.com • 1-800-784-9553

The 99th Monkey
A Spiritual Journalist's Misadventures with Gurus, Messiahs, Sex, Psychedelics, and Other Consciousness-Raising Experiments
by Eliezer Sobel
312 pages $16.95

The Bad Driver's Handbook
Hundreds of Simple Maneuvers to Frustrate, Annoy, and Endanger Those Around You
by Zack Arnstein and
Larry Arnstein
192 pages $12.95

Calculated Risk
The Extraordinary Life of Jimmy Doolittle
by Jonna Doolittle Hoppes
360 pages $24.95

Captured!
Inside the World of Celebrity Trials
by Mona Shafer Edwards
176 pages $24.95

Creepy Crawls
A Horror Fiend's Travel Guide
by Leon Marcelo
384 pages $16.95

Dinner with a Cannibal
The Complete History of Mankind's Oldest Taboo
by Carole A. Travis-Henikoff
336 pages $24.95

Educating the Net Generation
How to Engage Students in the 21st Century
by Bob Pletka, Ed.D.
192 pages $16.95

The Encyclopedia of Sixties Cool
A Celebration of the Grooviest People, Events, and Artifacts of the 1960s
by Chris Strodder
336 pages $24.95

Exotic Travel Destinations for Families
by Jennifer M. Nichols and
Bill Nichols
360 pages $16.95

Footsteps in the Fog
Alfred Hitchcock's San Francisco
by Jeff Kraft and
Aaron Leventhal
240 pages $24.95

French for Le Snob
Adding Panache to Your Everyday Conversations
by Yvette Reche
400 pages $16.95

Haunted Hikes
Spine-Tingling Tales and Trails from North America's National Parks
by Andrea Lankford
376 pages $16.95

James Dean Died Here
The Locations of America's Pop Culture Landmarks
by Chris Epting
312 pages $16.95

L.A. Noir
The City as Character
by Alain Silver and
James Ursini
176 pages $19.95

Led Zeppelin Crashed Here
The Rock and Roll Landmarks of North America
by Chris Epting
336 pages $16.95

Movie Star Homes
by Judy Artunian and
Mike Oldham
312 pages $16.95

Redneck Haiku
Double-Wide Edition
by Mary K. Witte
240 pages $11.95

Route 66 Adventure Handbook
by Drew Knowles
312 pages $16.95

The Ruby Slippers, Madonna's Bra, and Einstein's Brain
The Locations of America's Pop Culture Artifacts
by Chris Epting
312 pages $16.95

Rudolph, Frosty, and Captain Kangaroo
The Musical Life of Hecky Krasnow—Producer of the World's Most Beloved Children's Songs
by Judy Gail Krasnow
424 pages $24.95

School Sense
How to Help Your Child Succeed in Elementary School
by Tiffani Chin, Ph.D.
408 pages $16.95

Self-Loathing for Beginners
by Lynn Phillips
216 pages $12.95

Silent Traces
Discovering Early Hollywood Through the Films of Charlie Chaplin
by John Bengtson
304 pages $24.95

The Sixties
Photographs by Robert Altman
192 pages $39.95

Tiki Road Trip
A Guide to Tiki Culture in North America
2nd Edition
by James Teitelbaum
360 pages $16.95

Tower Stories
An Oral History of 9/11
by Damon DiMarco
528 pages $27.95

The Ultimate Counterterrorist Home Companion
Six Incapacitating Holds Involving a Spatula and Other Ways to Protect Your Family
by Zack Arnstein and
Larry Arnstein
168 pages $12.95

"We're Going to See the Beatles!"
by Garry Berman
288 pages $16.95

Order Form 1-800-784-9553

	Quantity	Amount
The 99th Monkey ($16.95)	_____	_____
The Bad Driver's Handbook ($12.95)	_____	_____
Calculated Risk ($24.95)	_____	_____
Captured! ($24.95)	_____	_____
Creepy Crawls ($16.95)	_____	_____
Dinner with a Cannibal ($24.95)	_____	_____
Educating the Net Generation ($16.95)	_____	_____
The Encyclopedia of Sixties Cool ($24.95)	_____	_____
Exotic Travel Destinations for Families ($16.95)	_____	_____
Footsteps in the Fog ($24.95)	_____	_____
French for Le Snob ($16.95)	_____	_____
Haunted Hikes ($16.95)	_____	_____
James Dean Died Here ($16.95)	_____	_____
L.A. Noir ($19.95)	_____	_____
Led Zeppelin Crashed Here ($16.95)	_____	_____
Movie Star Homes ($16.95)	_____	_____
Redneck Haiku ($11.95)	_____	_____
Route 66 Adventure Handbook ($16.95)	_____	_____
The Ruby Slippers, Madonna's Bra, and Einstein's Brain ($16.95)	_____	_____
Rudolph, Frosty, and Captain Kangaroo ($24.95)	_____	_____
School Sense ($16.95)	_____	_____
Self-Loathing for Beginners ($12.95)	_____	_____
Silent Traces ($24.95)	_____	_____
The Sixties ($39.95)	_____	_____
Tiki Road Trip ($16.95)	_____	_____
Tower Stories ($27.95)	_____	_____
The Ultimate Counterterrorist Home Companion ($12.95)	_____	_____
"We're Going to See the Beatles!" ($16.95)	_____	_____

	Subtotal _____
Shipping & Handling: 1 book $4.00 Each additional book is $1.00	CA residents add 8.25% sales tax _____ Shipping and Handling (see left) _____ **TOTAL** _____

Name _____

Address _____

City _____ State _____ Zip _____

☐ Visa ☐ MasterCard Card No.: _____

Exp. Date _____ Signature _____

☐ Enclosed is my check or money order payable to:

Santa Monica Press LLC
P.O. Box 1076
Santa Monica, CA 90406

www.santamonicapress.com 1-800-784-9553